COLIN PORTER

Rowing to Win

STANLEY PAUL

London

STANLEY PAUL & CO. LTD
178–202 Great Portland Street, London, W.1

AN IMPRINT OF THE   HUTCHINSON GROUP

London Melbourne Sydney
Auckland Bombay Toronto
Johannesburg New York

★

First published 1959

*This book has been set in Bembo type face. It has
been printed in Great Britain by The Anchor Press,
Ltd., in Tiptree, Essex, on Antique Wove paper and
bound by Taylor Garnett Evans & Co., Ltd., in
Watford, Herts*

To

PAMELA DOWNES

who typed the manuscript, drew all the sketches, introduced some coherency into my writing and generally spent at least as much time on the book as I did.

Acknowledgements

I am indebted to Messrs. Geo. Bushell &
Son, the Associated Press Agency, the
Sport and General Press Agency, the Air
Ministry Photographic Unit and Bippa
for permission to reproduce the photographs illustrating this book; and to
Brigadier J. H. Gibbon, D.S.O., for the
loan of the photograph of the 1899
Cambridge crew. Both C. G. V. Davidge
and G. G. H. Page took considerable
pains over checking the manuscript and
I am very grateful for their assistance
and helpful advice.

Contents

Illustrations

Foreword

Many books have been written on the art of rowing—cynics will say too many—but never before has one been written by an oarsman who is still fully active in the field of both domestic and international rowing. Colin Porter needs no introduction to the rowing world. His racing career has been highly successful both at home and abroad, but he is always the first to study in detail the methods of other crews, particularly any which may have managed to beat him. Hence he can speak with greater weight than some authors whose experience of racing good foreign crews is largely confined to Henley Royal Regatta, and whose recollections of really high-class rowing and, in particular, racing may be somewhat dimmed by the passage of time, even if they ever had to face the competition which our crews do today.

Mr. Porter has been a highly controversial figure in the field of British Rowing. In certain circles he has been accused of exerting a deleterious influence by introducing a pseudo-American style and by preaching a gospel of fanatical fitness to the exclusion of all technique. That he is a much-maligned man is readily apparent from perusing this book. He does not introduce any new style of rowing, nor does he confuse his readers with a lengthy treatise on oarsmanship. He just picks out the sound basic essentials for moving a boat, and how refreshing it is to find this simple approach. One only has to talk to successful foreign oarsmen and coaches to discover that they also employ this approach. Anyone who attended the

European Championships at Duisburg or Posnan can hardly have ascribed the three gold medals won by Germany's crews to their great skill or experience. In fact it was quite frightening to an Englishman to see what rough crews could win with relative ease. However rough they may have looked, not only had they been firmly grounded in the fundamentals of boat propulsion, but they had been so carefully and scientifically trained that they could maintain an absolutely ruthless pressure without losing their basic form throughout a race. The absence of this is painfully obvious in most English crews.

There is another aspect of rowing which one sees on the Continent, and particularly in the U.S.A., and that is the great attention paid to working out the strategy and psychology of racing and to the building up of a fantastic fighting spirit. One of our greatest difficulties in this respect is that we have not yet got in this country the straight 2,000-metre courses on still water which exist both in Europe and America on which four, five, six or sometimes as many as ten crews can, and frequently do, race abreast. There is no doubt that this type of racing, done half a dozen or more times in the season, gives that extra turn of speed which so often beats an English crew of equal or superior technique.

Mr. Porter devotes a considerable amount of his book to this much neglected aspect of rowing but at the same time is careful to point out that first-class technique and experience are of the greatest importance. A recent crew which has impressed me as displaying a fine combination of all these assets is the Italian VIII from the Cannottieri Moto Guzzi, winners of the European Championships for the last two years. Their crew had a great wealth of experience in international rowing—one of them first won an Olympic Gold Medal in 1948 and has been in the forefront of international rowing ever since. Whatever may be the advantages of their curious rig, their technique and skill were superb by any standards, largely a product of their great experience. There have been English crews of equal skill and possibly equal experience, but on top of this the Italians had undertaken a most rigorous and scientific training both for fitness and racing technique. This appeared to follow the methods adopted by many of the world's leading middle-distance runners.

Mr. Porter himself has experimented with such methods both as an oarsman and as a coach—not without a fair measure of success. But he would be the first to admit that he and others who have studied these methods still have a great deal to learn about them and are still faced with the far greater problem of putting them into practice. Many experts will disagree with the suggestions made, but few will deny that there is a very real need for further experiment with training and racing technique, apart from trying to improve the standard of oarsmanship. They must both be tackled. The one will not succeed without the other.

Finally, I am not at all certain that there is not something else slightly lacking in the attitude of many English oarsmen. An old rowing man of some distinction said to a friend of mine at Henley this year, 'Oh well, they think of nothing else but winning races.' He was criticizing the club for which Mr. Porter rowed this season. I like to think that that remark inspired the title of this book.

CHRISTOPHER DAVIDGE
September 1958

Introduction

I am well aware of the hazards to be encountered in writing a book on rowing, particularly at the present time when new ideas and new methods are sweeping through all the competitive sports leaving behind a succession of broken records and conflicting dogmas. 'What is wrong with British rowing?' you ask, and everyone rushes forward with a solution—State support, harder training, different equipment, better technique, etc.; in these circumstances what chance is there that one can find even two people who agree completely?

Yet one of the things that has struck me again and again is that although the arguments rage backwards and forwards, few of the protagonists differ much as far as the essentials are concerned: everyone is far too busy killing dragons that do not exist (probably they never did). All coaches are glad to have big, strong men in their crews, and I have yet to hear one that did not at least pay lip-service to fitness and the need for solid bladework, hard beginnings and clean finishes. The differences to be found lie not in the fundamentals themselves but in the relative emphasis placed on each.

What I have tried to do is to treat the science of rowing as a whole rather than to deal with only one feature of it (such as technique) on the tacit assumption that this gives the complete picture. To do this properly it is important to keep an open mind and to present all points of view even whilst stating one's own preferences, but in spite of all my good resolutions I dare say that touches of prejudice will show through now and again.

Basically it is the material that counts and a club having a plentiful supply of large young men with the right approach can hardly help but do better than one which has not, no matter what else they believe in; the problem is how to make the best of what is available. This is one of the reasons why I have drawn my examples from the R.A.F. Rowing Club rather than from the other and bigger clubs for which I have rowed. During the time that I was stationed at Benson our membership was rarely more than a dozen; the men were not particularly large, strong or experienced and came from different clubs all over the country; we had little money and secondhand boats, moreover we had to arrange our training with regard to the unusual demands of an armed service where some of the crew were liable to be on duty all night or over the weekend. What was achieved by these crews is no more than could be done by any other small club.

Regarding the title I have no apology to make; my attitude to rowing has always been that I row to race and I race to win: it is the only one consistent with the use of racing boats. When the boatbuilder turns out a new shell he has done everything he can to make it fast; in lightness and in streamlining he can do no more, and if there are those who profess to row for the exercise or to work up a thirst the least they can do is to leave the racing boats to those who intend to race, for there are other and more leisurely ways of taking exercise on the water.

The true enjoyment of rowing lies in racing—from the crew of young boys thrashing along in a tub IV, to the wily septuagenarian using all the tricks of the trade to stay ahead of them in a sculling boat. Nor can it be denied that the object of racing is to win. Whatever the type of boat, whatever the standard of the opposition—get to the winning post first! This is the other reason why I quote so often from the R.A.F. crews—they had an all-pervading urge to win at any cost and I think this was because we paid more attention than most clubs to the development of killer instinct.

The inculcation of a ruthless racing spirit can be as important a factor as any in getting the optimum performance from an oarsman or crew, yet it is often neglected altogether. In this book I have tried not only to discuss the various physical aspects of rowing but, by drawing frequently on my Air Force days, to give some idea of what I think the mental outlook of an oarsman should be if he is going to succeed. If in doing so I give the impression that rowing on these terms is a grim, humourless sport then you must believe me when I say it is not; I have never enjoyed my rowing more than when the pace has been hottest and the training most gruelling and I am sure that the same went for my fellow-oarsmen. If support is needed for this statement it can be said that the majority of them returned to their own clubs, when their service was over, to instil the same spirit there—often with remarkable results—and that as I write now (1958), some four or five years later, many of these ex-R.A.F. oarsmen are still in the front line of British rowing.

Any volume of this sort is certain to be largely autobiographical, as one is only really safe treading on the firm ground of personal experience. My own rowing has been chiefly with small clubs of limited membership and facilities and so I suppose it is natural that this book was written mainly with the small club in mind. Other, and better qualified, authors than I have written for the university oarsman, many have dealt solely with technique and others have directed their remarks primarily to coaches. But I have found numerous small clubs, with only a handful of enthusiasts, that are looking for a way to pull themselves up by their shoe-strings and their needs are more comprehensive. In many cases it is only too easy for them to acquire a narrow-minded outlook on rowing and to be unable to rise above a very low standard, yet I see the makings of crews which might represent Great Britain with success if they could only get the whole picture into perspective and appreciate what they themselves are capable of if they set about it in the right way.

I remember my first championship race in 1953; we were a small, young, inexperienced IV chosen, much to our surprise, to represent the country after winning the Wyfolds at Henley. Brought up to believe in our own limitations we did not see how we could be of international class. There we were, drawn in the first heat against Belgium, Austria and Jugoslavia—the latter with exactly the same crew that had won at the Olympic Games in Helsinki the year before. Speaking for myself I rowed practically the whole race with my eyes shut praying that we would not be left too far behind, and when I looked up near the finish we were winning. My eyes were opened in both senses and I realized then what lay within the grasp of any sufficiently determined crew.

The National Provincial Bank crew which I had the pleasure of coaching in 1957 did much the same thing. Averaging barely eleven stone, not one of them had won a senior rowing event at the start of the season, yet they romped home in the Wyfolds and reached the final of the Thames Cup at Henley; being selected to represent Great Britain in the European Championships they got to the final of the coxless IVs. Three members of the VIII and one of the IV had only started rowing the previous year and when, at the beginning of the summer, I talked about the European Championships, they all thought I was joking.

This, then, is my ulterior motive: to try to persuade the average club oarsman that he has it in him to climb above the standard that he tends to set himself and, if he is prepared to condition himself mentally and physically, to break into the infinitely rewarding field of international rowing. If enough oarsmen can acquire the confidence to do this, then the whole standard of British rowing will be forced up.

I

First Steps

The right approach

WHY do young people take up rowing, as opposed to other sports which may be cheaper, less physically exacting and needing to be practised only when the inclination is there? Many row because they are not very good at anything else, some because their fathers rowed before them and others because their friends seem to enjoy it. Some people are never happier than when they are near, on or in the water, and rowing is a 'natural' to them, and yet others start rowing at school in order to avoid playing or watching cricket. Whatever the reason, rowing can give such transcendent pleasure that it has the power to transform the hesitant novice into the ardent enthusiast.

In many ways it is as well that the newcomer does not realize what he is in for. He may have other interests and hobbies—inexorably these will be pushed out of the way; he may like to go away for the occasional weekend—he will not get the chance; he may not contemplate coming back from a row so exhausted that he has to sit on the landing-stage to put his shoes on—he will find this commonplace. Yet there are compensations which at the beginning he cannot comprehend: the infinite delight of an immaculate row; the satisfaction of beating one's fellows; the aesthetic pleasure of the sun rippling off the water, of flexing wood and the wind on his back. Ere long he will grow nostalgic for the flapping of white canvas in the breeze that betokens regatta time, and the smell of varnish hot in the sun.

But first he must learn the elements of rowing, and the maxim for the beginner is 'do not rush'. Do not rush on to the indoor tank and there race up and down the slide; do not rush to get out in the tub pair; do not rush to get a seat in the VIII. Paradoxically, the slower he is to move from step to step the sooner he will become a competent oarsman.

The very first step of all is to watch a capable oarsman rowing in the bank tub or indoor tank. Notice all the movements he makes to manipulate the oar, how he drops the inside wrist at the finish to bring the oar on to the feather, how he lets his hands come up as he slides forward to bring the blade down to the water; above all, notice how he slows down as he approaches the beginning of the stroke. Now try it out, taking it steadily; do everything in slow motion, not trying to row the oar through the water at all. Ask the experienced oarsman to help you and correct your movements when you go wrong, then sit and practise by the hour for as long as they will let you, for it is much easier to learn the movements in rowing in the fixed tank than it is in a moving boat.

When I started rowing at school I think I was very lucky in that the boat club was just getting going again after the war; all the equipment was in need of repair and we had to get down and do it ourselves. The tank was the first thing we reconditioned and for several weeks, while we varnished the tub pair, we took it in turns each day to practise in it. Then the tub was ready and for several weeks we were necessarily confined to that. By the time we had the outrigged boats repaired we were all reasonably competent, and so we learnt to handle the lighter craft that much quicker. I am sure that because of the limitations of gear we all learnt to row better in a shorter time than those who came after us and were taking out the racing boats within their first month.

Once the oar can be handled correctly and the forward

movement is fairly smooth then the beginner can venture out on the water, but he should never hesitate to return to the bank tub or tank to practise individual points, even after he has progressed to outrigged craft and racing boats.

Equipment

Clearly the first thing to do when we are asked to tackle a job is to examine the tools we are given to use. The novice's initial approach to the river will be via the tub pair, which we will assume is lying afloat beside the landing-stage. If the row-lock is on the nearside of the boat the oar should be placed into it and the swivel tightened first, the oar then being left balanced across the boat; if the rowlock is on the far side, place the oar across the boat with the narrow part of the loom next to the swivel. The importance of this drill, which is the same for any class of boat, is that if a wash hits it while your attention is distracted, no damage to the fragile blade will result. Next to consider getting into the boat—an action which often gives a clue to the oarsman's potentiality; grasp the saxboard firmly with one hand on each side and, taking all the weight on your hands, place your foot carefully on to the centre board if the boat has footboards, or on to the front carriage of the slide if it has not. The other foot then goes straight on to the stretcher or into the clog, and only then do you transfer your weight from the hands to the seat.

There is a particularly tricky apparatus which is popular at garden fêtes and which consists of a large, open wooden box suspended on a pole running horizontally through the middle of it. To win a prize the contestant has to climb into the box and, with the aid of a punt pole, balance it for a specified period without touching the ground. It is a good idea to treat a boat in the same way when you are getting in: try to imagine that it will roll over if your weight is not always balanced over the keel (as indeed it would if it were not for the oars, or someone holding the rigger). I have seen some so-called Grand Class oarsmen getting into a boat as if they were old women going down stairs, and it is a sure sign that their watermanship is poor.

Once in and settled the first thing to do is to fasten your oar in the rowlock if you have not already done so and push it outwards until the button is seated against the thole pin. I like to do this as soon after I am in the boat as possible, as I have seen too many people take unwanted duckings when relying

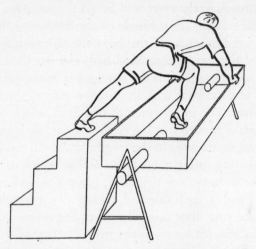

Think of this when you step into a boat

on some chap who was *supposed* to be holding the rigger! Perhaps I have a distrustful nature, but between entrusting my person to the boat and securing the oar, my dry condition is someone else's responsibility and I like this period to be very short.

Next, the stretcher: this will either be fitted with straps, in which case you will normally wear shoes in the boat, or with clogs, which are primitively constructed shoes made from three strips of leather, in which case you step into the boat in your stockinged feet. If the person who used the boat before you had small feet or thin socks you will have to undo the straps and laces before you can get your feet into the clogs.

Assuming the novice is of normal stature, and the boat is fitted with a standard eighteen-inch, or less, slide, the simplest method of adjusting the stretcher is to undo the thumb-screws, sit at the backstop and gently push the knees down flat. The stretcher should be fixed so that when the knees are flat and the body is upright there is a slight pressure between the stretcher and the backstop. Many coaches will tell crew members to set their stretchers by their frontstops or by the angle of the blade on the beginning, but I believe that the average man is adequately served—at least to begin with—by setting his stretcher as described.

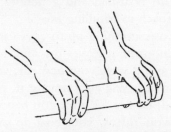

Hold the oar with the fingers

Next, there is the oar, which is as important to the oarsman as the golf club is to the golfer. No golfer who aspires to competition will tolerate a badly balanced club or will take hold of it anyhow, nor should the oarsman his oar. The leather should be well greased and the handle shaved to a manageable size. My experience of English clubs is that nearly all oarsmen learn to row with far too large an oar handle. They start rowing with it, get used to it and refuse to try anything else, when actually it stiffens up the muscles in the forearm, is harder to manipulate and more easily knocked out of the hand by rough water. A good guide is to take hold of the oar normally and squeeze the fingers and thumb together round the handle; if the thumbnail half overlaps the nail of the longest finger then the handle is small enough, if not—have it shaved down. Hold the oar with the fingers rather than in the palm, leaving about four inches between the hands. On no account should the oar be gripped tightly or the forearms will stiffen up. Remember that only relaxed muscles can act quickly.

Finally, a word about care of equipment. The great majority of oarsmen are far too careless in handling boats and oars, and though it is frequently deplored this slackness still prevails. Possibly it is partly because most colleges and the larger clubs have boatmen to carry out repairs for them. This is very useful but it does tend to produce an unconcerned attitude in the oarsman. A good deal of my rowing was done at clubs having no boatman and generally I found there a much better approach to handling boats.

A new boat costs anything up to £350 and it is literally a shell. From the moment it leaves the rack to the moment it returns cherish it as if it were your new car; watch that you do not hit anything while you are carrying it, particularly when swinging it round; do not let go if you happen to slip on the landing-stage; if you 'throw' your boat do so together or you may damage the bows or the rudder. While on the water keep a sharp lookout for other boats and floating debris—a sheet of ice just submerged has sunk an VIII before now. When launching a boat hold it well clear of the stage, in case of bolt-heads and other projections; watch out for submerged piles; when there are launches about or the water is rough hold the boat a foot clear of the stage the whole time until you are ready to push off. In many ways I wish all oarsmen were made to do their own repairs for the first year or two, perhaps they would then realize how long it takes to put a tingle in a boat or to re-cover the canvasses.

The beginning

Almost as soon as I start to describe the actions of rowing I am in danger of plunging into the stormy waters of controversy, but I will try to avoid doing so in this chapter at least. By 'the beginning' is meant the beginning of the stroke through the water, for let it be stressed at the outset that rowing is a cycle where every action depends to some extent on the one before it.

For the first few strokes the novice can do no better than to sit and take a few jabs at the water, watching the blade and building up a mental relationship between what he does with the handle and what happens at the other end. As the weeks go by and the miles mount up, this association will improve until every action becomes instinctive and the oarsman can tell, solely by the feel of the oar, whether he is late or early, whether his blade is at the right depth and, ultimately, even how fast the boat is travelling.

The prime object of the beginning is to lock the oar in the water so that it can be used to lever the boat along. But since the boat is moving, it is not just a case of raising the oar handle and letting the blade drop into the water—if this were done, as soon as the very tip of the blade touched the water some would be splashed towards the bows of the boat producing a 'back-splash', as it is called, and checking its speed.

To prepare for a good beginning the blade should be brought down to the water (unless it is rough) and there should be a distinct deceleration as the slide approaches the frontstop, for if the blade is six inches off the water when the beginning is taken the oarsman is going to miss twice as much length on the beginning as he need, and if he does not slow down he is unlikely to co-ordinate the thrust from the stretcher with the blade gripping the water.

Because the human spring is fully wound at the beginning it is natural to recoil off the stretcher and this often results in the reverse of the 'back-splash'; that is, the blade overtakes the water as it descends and more of the stroke has been rowed by the time it is fully covered than is strictly necessary. We call it 'rowing the blade into the water'.

This matter of timing the vertical lift of the handle with

the horizontal thrust of the legs and body is the whole secret of a good beginning and, generally, of a good stroke.

Since the inexperienced oarsman can more often get away with rowing his blade into the water and losing some of his length behind the rigger rather than 'back-splashing' (which shows up all too clearly and is generally more difficult to achieve), the former is a good deal more common. However much an oarsman rows his blade in he should realize that one of the tasks he must work at is to catch hold of the water more and more quickly, and that means a faster and faster lift of the hands on the beginning.

I have talked about 'catching the water' and 'locking the blade' without really explaining these terms. Obviously the act of putting the blade in at the same speed as the water passing the boat is not by itself going to provide any impetus and it must be followed instantly by a tremendous thrust with the legs against the stretcher, coupled with a backward swing of the shoulders and draw with the arms. The driving of the blade against the water causes a mound to build up in front of it and it is this mound which provides the resistance against which to lever the boat along. This is what is meant by 'locking the blade'.

The finish

Why jump straight from the beginning to the finish without describing the stroke itself? The reason is that if the beginning is correctly executed the middle of the stroke becomes very straightforward: it is, quite simply, the driving forward of the boat by all the power of legs, body and arms that the oarsman can command.

Ideally the finish of the stroke should coincide with the finish of the leg drive, the finish of the body swing and the finish of the arm draw. Normally the sequence of finishing is more likely to be legs, body and finally arms, since that is the relative order of strength of these three sets of muscles.

The flattening of the knees and the drawing in of the oar handle to touch the body betoken their own completion, and only one question remains: how far back should the body swing be carried? I do not want to discuss this point at length in this chapter, and the best guide for the beginner is to carry the finish through to the point where it is no longer possible to apply full power to the blade. Plates I and II (opposite page 32) show, respectively, an R.A.F. VIII at an early stage of training during the 'Conibear' season (1953), and the Cambridge VIII just before the Boat Race in 1952. Most crews

Balanced between stretcher and oar handle
supposing the seat to be removed

will achieve a compromise somewhere between these two extremes.

For a good finish I like to imagine that a fraction of a second before the blade is struck out of the water the oarsman is still balanced solely between stretcher and oar handle. If the oarsman feels that he would drop through the bottom of the boat if someone removed the seat at this instant then he is probably lying back too far.

The manipulation of the oar at the finish becomes so instinctive that it is difficult to analyse. Essentially it is the outside hand that strikes the handle down and the wrist of the inside hand that drops slightly, starting the oar on to the feather, and the oar is generally allowed to roll under the palm of the inside hand and the fingers of the outside hand until it is fully feathered.

Transferring the attention to what is happening at the blade end: the back of the blade should follow tangentially the arc that is the downward and forward movement of the oar. If that sounds complicated perhaps a sketch will help to explain it.

Hard finish—blade square as it leaves the water

This is the ideal for which to strive and, as the blade actually leaves the water square, it follows that the finish must be rowed through hard. What more often happens is that the oarsman feathers his oar slightly and uses the speed of the boat to help lift his oar out for him. This enables him to row a weak finish and still extract his blade cleanly; however, it uses up some of the speed of the boat and so detracts from the run.

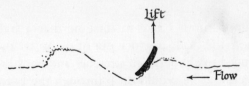

Lazy finish—using the pressure of the water on the back of a partly feathered blade to lift it out

Going back to the ideal finish it may be thought that, as with the beginning, the blade must be lifted out during the last piece of the stroke if it is to move at the same speed as the water and, of course, this would cause loss of length at the finish. Nevertheless, this is not strictly necessary since a blade rowed through hard to the finish will have an air space behind it and if the blade is lifted out quickly enough the water will not have time to rush in and strike the back of it. The important thing about the finish is not to be frightened of it (and the thought of a rigid oar anchored at the far end and moving rapidly in the direction of one's stomach can be disquieting) as any hesitation just before the finish will allow water to fill the air space behind the blade, and it will be harder than ever to remove the oar cleanly.

I had a dramatic experience of this once when I was rowing in a London University crew. My finish had been giving me trouble and I seemed quite incapable of getting the oar out without throwing up a plume of water; our coach was 'referring' to my finish more and more often and I was getting rather frantic. Inevitably, I lost my temper both with it and the coach and threw all my weight on to the oar, making no effort to get it out—I felt sure it would get firmly stuck, causing me to catch a monumental crab and, with any luck, splitting the boat in two. But, apparently of its own accord, the oar came out square and true. The moral is clear— the harder you row the finish, the easier it is to get the blade out.

Coming forward

This part of the stroke—when the oarsman is preparing to drive the boat again—is frequently called the 'recovery'. At a normal racing gait twice as much time will be spent coming forward as going back, and since the boat will not then be accelerating, the whole essence of coming forward should be relaxation; it is the vital period of rest before the next onslaught on the water.

If the finish has been correctly executed the hands will be moving down and away over the thighs. When the arms have straightened, the body will swing as far as it is going to and, lastly, the slide will be drawn up. This time-honoured sequence is still valid for very obvious reasons. If, for instance, the knees are brought up before the hands have passed over them they will impede the forward movement of the oar. The hands are the logical start of the forward movement since they complete the finish, besides being the lightest and most easily manipulated of the three muscle groups. There are other good reasons for completing the hand and body movements as quickly as possible, for when the oarsman is sitting back his weight is entirely on his seat, but as he swings forward some of his weight is transferred to his stretcher and he is in a better position to control the boat.

One way in which I like to think of the forward movement is to imagine that the blade is following the correct arc, motivated by some external force, and that the oarsman is completely relaxed, holding on to the oar handle and being pulled forward by it. If this were to happen the arms would be pulled straight first, the body dragged forward next and, finally, the seat drawn up.

As far as the relative speed is concerned the handle should be whipped round and away over the ankles as quickly as possible until the oarsman is in a position of control: that is, with some of his weight planted firmly on the stretcher. Then, as the last of the swing blends smoothly into the start of the slide, so everything steadies up, the pressure on the stretcher increasing as the human spring winds up and the last few inches of the slide completely under control as the oarsman prepares himself to take the next stroke.

In subdividing movements into different muscle groups it is difficult to avoid the impression that there is a sharp dividing line between, say, the finish of the swing and the commencement of the slide, but of course this is not so. As the arms become nearly straight the body will start to swing over, and as the swing nears completion so the slide will start to move. With practice all these muscle groups blend in together to give

PLATE I

SHORT FINISH

R.A.F. VIII in training, January 1953

PLATE II

LONG FINISH

The Cambridge crew of 1952 at Putney. 'Most crews will achieve a compromise somewhere between these two extremes.' (page 29)

PLATE III

R.A.F. VIII, January 1953

'Some obviously weak positions.' (page 36)

an impression of such fluid movement that it is impossible to say when one action finishes and the next starts.

If the oar handle has been rolled down and away over the thighs at the finish of the stroke, and the blade is to be brought down squared to the water for the beginning, the oar handle must actually travel through an arc something like this:

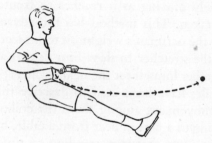

The forward arc

One can combine this last half of the forward swing with an exercise in relaxation, by allowing the pressure of the hands on the handle to be so light that the outboard weight of the oar causes the handle to rise slowly as it moves forward over the stretcher, bringing the blade down to the water.

As the hands come over the stretcher so the oar is turned square. With practice this action becomes quite automatic and involves very little physical effort. The oar is actually rolled into the squared position between the thumb and the balls of the fingers of the inside hand, the handle turning freely under the fingers of the outside hand.

A good oarsman will modify his height of feathering and time of squaring to suit the conditions. If the water is rough the blade should be kept high on the feather until the last minute and then brought down for the beginning in a wide sweep. In a headwind it pays to square the blade as late as possible in order to cut down wind resistance and save effort in coming forward. If, in addition, the water is calm the blade feathered near the water is less likely to catch the wind.

Generally, in English rowing the tempo of the forward movement is rapid at first, slowing down as the oarsman approaches the beginning. That is, the hands come away quickly and the body swings over without checking. The slide comes fairly fast off the backstop and slows down uniformly until it is barely moving as it reaches to frontstops and the beginning is taken. This method has the advantage both of concentrating the oarsman's weight on to his feet (which must press against the stretcher to slow him down) and also gives him time to gather himself for the next stroke.

Many similes have been used to describe this last part of the forward movement, among them the coiling of a spring and the grasping of a pint of beer from a table, but my preference is for imagining that I am standing on tiptoe holding an umbrella by the ferrule and reaching out and up to hook the handle over a hatstand. To me this mind-picture symbolizes the loose, easy reaching for the beginning.

A loose, easy reach

Early faults

Most early faults come from a feeling of insecurity, and when you think of it there are few places of greater insecurity than a racing boat. It moves forward (and sideways) on the water; it also rolls very easily; the oar handle is not fixed and can move in any direction except outwards; the seat moves and, as soon as you touch it, the water moves too!

For this reason many early faults would never arise if all oarsmen were to be given a thorough grounding on the indoor tank and then the tub pair before they were put in a fully outrigged boat. I wish club captains would realize just how much more difficult it is to learn to row when the boat is unsteady: one stroke the novice comes forward with his blade slobbering along the water, the next it is way up in the air, yet he is expected to get a quick beginning, row his blade through level, and come out cleanly at the finish—a task that would tax even an experienced man. If every novice were to be made to put in twenty hours on the tank before being allowed near a boat, and another forty hours in a tub pair plus a further twenty hours tanking before being allowed out in an outrigger, he would be a competent oarsman in a fraction of the time it would otherwise take.

The first thing a beginner will do when put in the tank is to come racing forward, pull his blade through the water, laboriously struggle to get it out and, once it is safely clear, race forward to have another shot. This fundamental anxiety to get on with the next stroke persists for a long time unless it is checked in the early days. An oarsman must learn that a lot of thought goes into a good stroke and that gathering over the stretcher and preparing for the beginning is half the battle. Until he has learnt the knack of dropping his inside wrist and, at the same time, striking the handle down with the outside hand the novice will take some time getting getting his oar out at the finish. This means that the 'follow through' of the hands—body—slide will be lost and, finding himself faced

35

with the task of coming forward again, he will probably pull himself up by his shoe-straps until his slide hits the frontstop, throwing his shoulders forward and down. Apart from knocking him off balance this usually has the effect of making him sky his blade into the bargain. The cure is to concentrate on letting the hands lead and, if necessary, to make an exercise of holding the knees down until the hands and body have swung away forward.

Another major fault arising from insecurity is the tendency to lean to one side or the other either on the recovery because the boat is rolling, or during the stroke itself because there is an unequal thrust from the legs, or by twisting away from the oar at the finish. Easy as it is to say, and hard as it is to do, the whole secret of combating a rolling boat is to relax. Supposing the boat rolls to strokeside halfway forward, if the strokeside oarsmen are tense they will never be able to move their hands up or down quickly enough to absorb the shock and what usually happens is that their blades hit the water and knock the boat straight over on to bowside, and so it goes on.

Relaxing becomes even more important in rough water where the clearance of the oars is reduced, and one can always tell if an oarsman is properly relaxed or not when his blade hits a wave-top. If he is relaxed his blade will be knocked up into the air, if he is tense the whole boat will be knocked over on to the other side.

Good rowing requires the perfect co-ordination of several different muscle groups and it is very unlikely that this will be possible for the beginner. (Plate III, for example, shows an R.A.F. crew in the middle of the stroke. [*See* opposite page 33.] Each oarsman has applied his power in a different way and some have arrived in an obviously weak position.) If it so happens that all the muscle groups used in rowing have been developed to the same extent before he takes it up he will be referred to as a 'natural oar', but this is rare and does not mean he will be any better in the end than the man who has to strengthen certain groups of muscles by practice. The leg drive is nearly always strongest and will sometimes cause the slide to be shot to the backstop before the arms and trunk have started to play their parts, and sometimes even before the blade is solid in the water. To some degree this is inevitable and I believe that it can only be overcome by practice, until the stomach and back muscles are equally developed. Timing the entry of the blade, with the simultaneous application of all the muscle groups, is something requiring concentration by the oarsman, patience by the coach and many miles of water covered in practice.

The three S's: Strength, Stamina and Skill

The requirements of pace in a boat can be summarized by what I call the three S's—Strength, Stamina and Skill—and all three are necessary in some degree if an oarsman or crew is to acquire pace in a boat.

Strength appears an obvious requirement yet is too often neglected when it comes to selection. Strength, acquired by effort and practice, is the raw material that wins races. Look for the man that can bend his oar when he is rowing, no matter how rough and ungainly his action, for he is worth his place in any boat.

Stamina is the ability to keep applying one's strength to moving the boat every stroke without diminution as long as the race lasts. One may have strength before starting to row and one may be able to acquire skill quickly, but stamina must be built up over the months by repeatedly driving the body to keep going when it is tired. Of the three S's stamina is possibly the hardest to acquire; it is also the most easily lost when the oarsman stops rowing for a time. Lack of stamina manifests itself in a large time difference between the first and second halves of the course, and the often ragged appearance of a crew at the end of a race.

Skill is the harnessing of strength to moving the boat. The

more skilful the oarsman the more value he will get in terms of boat speed for the amount of effort he puts in. One can include technique, and therefore style, as components of skill, although the style adopted by some crews might not be considered as revealing skill by coaches of other schools!

Probably fewer races are won mainly by skill than are won mainly by strength or stamina, perhaps because skill is basically an instrument of transmission in transferring the intrinsic power of the human body to propelling a boat. Nevertheless, when it comes to the selection of oarsmen or crews skill is very often placed highest on the list; perhaps that explains why the critics are so often wrong when they forecast the results of races. I personally have come in for a good deal of criticism on the subject of technique and many coaches who have not had much contact with me accuse me of saying, or implying, that good technique is not essential to good rowing. Anyone who has read the preceding sentences may feel that there is some justification for this.

Let me state here and now that this is untrue; anybody who imagines they can get away with faulty technique or, indeed, without striving for more precision each outing, is making a mistake that will all too soon become obvious. The most intense coaching for technique I ever received was in the R.A.F. crews when, for most of the time, we had no coach outside the boat. I say this in spite of the excellent coaching I have received at other times. It may sound nonsense but will be readily appreciated by anyone who rowed in the R.A.F. crews of those times. We covered many hundreds of miles and all the time there was incessant coaching from within the boat.

Coaches sometimes tend to be tolerant of individual faults: having pointed out that '4' is late or '2' is rowing light they are apt to give him a break, perhaps assuming that he is doing his best or is incapable of improvement. Not the R.A.F. crews; there is no more ruthless coach than the man rowing behind you, your faults mean that his efforts are to some extent nullified, and as he is putting out as much effort as you are he feels, unlike the coach on the bank, that he is justified in driving his comments home stroke after stroke, mile after mile, outing after outing.

There is some danger in coaching from within the crew inasmuch as when oarsmen are tired, tempers become frayed and rows are apt to break out; for this reason a coach outside the boat is generally more desirable.

Whatever particular method of rowing is preferred the basic essentials of skill are the same the world over and there are certain symptoms which are rarely seen in really good crews. Such things, for instance, as slow beginnings, washy blades, dirty finishes, uncontrolled sliding and poor timing are seldom exhibited by first-class crews. The eradication of such faults must be the aim of every oarsman.

Some crews have been misled in the past into thinking that improvement in skill is not important and such crews have often gone thrashing up and down the river under the impression that that was all that was needed, but they have never achieved real pace. International standard is never likely to be realized without a proper balance between the three essentials—strength, stamina and skill.

2

Technique

What is style?

THE word 'style' as applied to rowing is anathema to many oarsmen; there is no such thing as style, they say. Indeed, some may remember a debate at Maidenhead a few years ago on the motion that 'British crews should adopt the Conibear style' which was defeated mainly because a number of people got up and argued that there was no such thing as the Conibear style and that therefore the motion was meaningless. It is true that the Americans themselves do not talk of the Conibear style but rather of the Harvard stroke or the Washington stroke, but to us nearly all American crews are similar in appearance, rig and technique, and it is, therefore, justifiable for us to talk of the Conibear style even if they would not do so.

I find that one of the dictionary definitions of style is the 'characteristic or peculiar mode of expression and execution', and this is what I mean when I refer to style in rowing. If anyone comes to me and says there is no such thing as the Conibear style they will find me unsympathetic; the measure by which the appearance and technique of a Russian crew differs from that of an American crew is that of the difference in their styles. This is the meaning I give to the word and this is the sense in which I shall use it even if it means offending the purists.

By style, then, I mean largely the technique of rowing;

and if I talk about, for instance, the Lady Margaret style, I mean the particular variation that has come to be associated with crews from that boat club and the coaching of the late Roy Meldrum—that is, the very long stroke through the water coupled with a pronounced body swing and consequently a somewhat low rate of striking.

There are an infinite number of variations of style, of course, but it is surprising how easy it is to give precise classifications to the best crews. The Cambridge colleges, for example, are generally equally endowed: each rows on the same stretch of water and draws on much the same sort of material. Yet since the war, at least, two colleges have stood out beyond the rest—Jesus and L.M.B.C.; both have won the Grand once and the Ladies' Plate two or three times at Henley, for instance. No one would deny, however, that they are at opposite ends of the range of variations in style: one sacrificing efficiency to economy of effort and the other economy to efficiency. Moreover, each is hard put to it to explain the success of its rivals.

Economy or efficiency

Having raised this question of economy and efficiency I will elaborate a bit further. When I use the word 'efficiency' I refer to the quantity of energy put into each stroke and hence the amount of impetus imparted by that one stroke. One can row a very efficient stroke by reaching far behind the rigger, catching the water at maximum reach, throwing all one's weight on to the oar and continuing to draw at it until it is physically impossible to swing back any further. Such a stroke will accelerate the boat a good deal, but it is hardly economical; it will use up much more energy than if the oarsman had rowed his blade into the water or finished the stroke but little past the vertical.

Similarly, when I talk about economy I do not necessarily mean that no energy is wasted, but rather that each individual stroke does not demand a very high output of energy and therefore does not impart as much acceleration to the boat. An oarsman who only reaches out as far as is comfortable, develops momentum with the oar by rowing it into the water and finishes upright, has rowed an economical stroke, but he has not built up his speed to the same extent as the ultra-efficient oarsman and, therefore, in order to maintain the same overall speed he will have to row at a higher rating and not allow his boat to slow down to quite the same extent. The following rough drawing shows the general pattern.

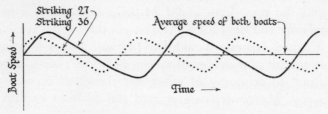

High-efficiency and low-efficiency crews

I think it is true to say that British crews generally attempt too high an efficiency in practice, compared with what they expect to produce during the race, and this shows itself in the large time differences, often amounting to fifteen seconds, between the first and second halves of the course at Henley, for example.

I am not going to say much about economy of effort as this is bound up with the physiology of the individual; it is a subject about which the medical profession is learning more and more and about which I certainly do not feel qualified to speak. I gather it is largely a question of what causes muscle fatigue and the way that this is bound up with speed of contraction of the muscle and the relative increase of fatigue with effort. But before going any further it would be as well to delve a little more deeply into the ways in which it is possible to increase the efficiency of a crew: that is, the amount of pace they are going to achieve per stroke. Efficiency can be developed both by training the oarsmen themselves, which I call physical efficiency, and also by alteration to the rig, which I deal with as mechanical efficiency.

Physical efficiency

No one has yet defined the limit of physical efficiency because this varies from oarsman to oarsman. Some oarsmen who are long in the arm and have supple shoulders can catch the water hard when the oar is at less than forty degrees to the boat without any undue strain; others cannot do this without straining to an extent which exhausts them rapidly; while others who are short or thickset could not even reach out so far. Again, famous oarsmen of the past have been able to row a hard finish with their shoulders practically on a level with the gunwale, where the strain on the stomach muscles would be intolerable for the majority.

It is possible to achieve considerable effective length without swinging far by being very quick to catch hold of the water at the beginning and very quick to clear the hands at the finish, so enabling pressure to be kept on the blade for as much of the rowing arc as possible.

Let us suppose, for instance, that just before the beginning the boat is moving at ten feet per second and that the blade is poised just above the water; ideally, in order to create no disturbance as it enters the water, the blade must actually travel towards the stern on entering. If it takes one-tenth of a second for the oarsman to cover his blade he will have rowed it exactly one foot horizontally before it is fully covered and can start to accelerate the boat; if he is able to drop his oar into the water in one-hundredth of a second he will only lose one-tenth of a foot and the effective length of his stroke will be increased by something like 10 per cent, assuming the arc of the blade relative to the boat to be about nine feet. Ideally, then, the blade should move into the water at an angle whose steepness depends on the speed of the boat and the degree of rapidity with which the oar handle can be raised, but in practice these movements tend to become rounded, sending the blade rather deeper into the water before it levels out. This action is generally all to the good as it is at the beginning of the stroke that the boat is moving slowest and the tendency for the blade to 'tear' is consequently greatest.

A similar reasoning will show that the length of stroke at the finish can also be increased purely by the speed with which the hands are struck down. Anyone who has not fully mastered the rapid downward thrust of the handle at the finish, coupled

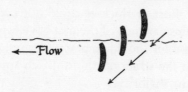

Angle of entry depends on the
relative speed of boat and catch

with the roll of the blade on to the feather, will have to begin the finish much earlier and this will result either in rowing the finish out of the water or else in letting the pressure off as he prepares to substitute a downward thrust of the hands for the horizontal draw.

Remembering my definition of efficiency as, simply, the amount of impetus given to the boat by each stroke, it is obvious that efficiency can be increased by rowing the blade through harder. Those who were at Henley in 1957 will remember a good example of this in the race between Ivanov and Mackenzie in the final of the Diamond Sculls. Over the bulk of the course Ivanov striking 28 and Mackenzie 30–31 maintained their relative positions, yet Mackenzie, the bigger and stronger man, was actually rowing the longer stroke.

Ivanov's efficiency came from his tremendous thrust through the water.

Mechanical efficiency

In addition to increasing the efficiency of a stroke by demanding greater effective length and power, it is possible to obtain greater efficiency purely by modification of the equipment used.

The mechanics of rowing may be examined from either of two standpoints: by regarding the oar as a lever of the first or second order. Without becoming technical one can consider the boat as static and the oar being used to lever water past it with the thole pin as fulcrum; or one can think of the water as being static and the boat being levered through the water by the pressure of the button on the thole pin, using the water as the fulcrum. The oarsman in the boat will generally find it easier to think of the first case, and the spectator on the bank or in the launch will probably prefer the second. Neither conception is entirely accurate as the true state of affairs lies somewhere between, depending on the degree of slip (or tear) of the blade in the water. Some degree of slip is inevitable since water is a yielding medium, and the amount of slip affects the efficiency of the stroke. Estimates of the amount of slip vary widely, but I believe that at a rate of about 30 with a 6-in. blade the average slip is about two feet at the tip. Many will undoubtedly disagree with me and I have heard six inches mentioned as a likely figure. My experience has been gained from just missing posts, buoys and floating objects while rowing, and I have found that I have to be at least two feet in front of a post, for example, on the beginning to avoid hitting it with my blade at the finish; this is assuming that my oar has been properly 'locked in' on the beginning and I have not rowed it in through the air.

Since blade-slip is caused by water flowing round the edges of the spoon it can obviously be reduced by enlarging the blade, so resulting in greater effective length of stroke. It might be thought advantageous to increase the width of the blade considerably but there are various disadvantages, and among these are:

1. Greater outboard weight.
2. Necessity for a greater vertical movement at beginning and finish in order to cover the blade and remove it cleanly.
3. If there was no slip at all anyone who was a fraction early on the beginning would soon break his oar (or his back!) so some blade-slip is desirable to 'cushion' the stroke.

Since 1 and 2 increase *pro rata* with the width of the blade, while the reduction in slip becomes smaller, a compromise is usually reached resulting in a blade width of between six and seven inches.

It is also possible to alter the effective length of the stroke by varying the leverage. Some oarsmen are easily put off by discussions on rig, and particularly leverage, but it is really very simple.

Strictly speaking, the leverage is:

$$\frac{\text{Overall length of oar}}{\text{Outboard length of oar}} = 1 + \frac{\text{Inboard length}}{\text{Outboard length}}.$$

In practice, the leverage is more often described as:

$$\frac{\text{Inboard length}}{\text{Outboard length}}.$$

The diagram shows examples somewhat exaggerated.

The smaller the leverage the greater the effective length of stroke—so it is possible to increase the length of stroke by shortening the distance between the handle and the button, and increasing that between the button and the blade. Supposing, for example, we have an oarsman whose physical reach (by which I mean the distance between his hands at the beginning and finish positions) is exactly five feet. If he uses an oar with a

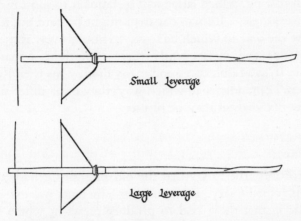

Inboard and outboard dimensions decide the
leverage

large leverage, such as 3 ft. 9 in. inboard and 8 ft. 2 in. outboard, his blade tip will travel 10 ft. 11 in. relative to the boat; whereas if his oar has a small leverage as, for instance, 3 ft. 7 in. inboard and 8 ft. 6 in. outboard, his blade arc will be 11 ft. 10 in. for the same 5-ft. reach; in this way the efficiency of his stroke will be increased by some 10 per cent.

Prominent styles

The degree to which efficiency or economy is stressed and, indeed, the various ways in which it is possible to achieve efficiency during the stroke, have resulted in the various styles which are seen in international competition today. I now propose to stick my neck out and give a brief description of the four styles of rowing which are, or have been, most prominent, and to endeavour to point out their advantages and disadvantages; in doing so I run the risk of having drawn some incorrect conclusions, particularly in the case of two of them where my personal experience has been very limited. At any rate, I will try to highlight the differences between them and modern English rowing, which latter will be familiar to most readers.

For example, a Russian oarsman might be hard put to it to describe the way in which he rows; to him his way is the only natural one and consequently there is nothing remarkable about it. If, as a result of a good many discussions with Russian oarsmen, I can indicate in which ways they think differently to us, then my analysis may be of use.

Orthodox

It is probably true to say that the old English Orthodox style is not practised today. The aim of its adherents was extremely laudable in that they tried to produce crews in which every man went through exactly the same motions and arrived at what was believed to be perfection in oarsmanship. This meant that not only had the bladework to be flawless but the movements of arms, body and legs had also to conform to the pattern believed to harness the most power to the oar handle: back held firm against the thrust of the legs (origin of the compliment that 'he rows with a straighter back than any other oarsman today'); head held up, eyes fixed ahead and looking slightly over the outside shoulder of the man in front; arms held straight out on the recovery and body swung right forward between the knees before the slide was allowed to move.

This rigid concept of oarsmanship led, not unnaturally, to a violent reaction which was particularly associated with Steve Fairbairn and his belief in natural action. The long and bitter

PLATE IV

VINTAGE ORTHODOX

Cambridge University at Bourne End, 1899

PLATE V

MODERN ORTHODOX

Leander Club beating Trinity College, Oxford, in a heat of the Grand Challenge Cup, Henley Royal Regatta, 1949

struggle between Orthodoxy and Fairbairnism was carried on up till the Second World War, and will be a source of amazement to oarsmen for the next two decades. Even now, the present-day oarsman is not clear what all the fuss was about.

Let there be no doubt why 'Orthodoxy', as it used to be, is dead. It was not killed by the ridicule of the Fairbairn extremists but by the one thing that will kill any system or style: lack of success. Whatever the adherents of Orthodoxy may claim, oarsmen are not fools and the only thing that can make them change their outlook is to be consistently beaten by someone who believes in and practises something else. We, by which I mean the modern generation, are asked to believe that the true stream of Orthodox rowing was from time to time tainted with deviations which resulted in the crews concerned going slower, but knowledge of human nature suggests that this was by no means the case. Oarsmen are not going to copy variations which will make them lose races.

The cause of this lack of success can be summed up in the phrase 'wastage of material'. Many extremely successful oarsmen row in a style peculiar to themselves: some with their knees together; some with a pronounced shoulder action; others take the catch with their arms. These mannerisms are often due to physical idiosyncrasies which were not taken into account by the old Orthodox school. More and more people took up rowing after reaching maturity, and these wanted to race without having to spend years in the physical development necessary for eventual conformity to Orthodox standards.

No doubt it will be denied that Orthodoxy, as I have described it, is dead, but what passes for Orthodoxy now is actually very little different from what has become the standard English style: that is, the coaching of the body only as far as its actions are detrimental to the bladework.

Plate V (opposite page 49) shows a heat of the Grand Challenge Cup in 1949 between Trinity College, Oxford, and Leander Club; if you were to look for vestiges of the Orthodox style you would surely expect to find them here in these two crews having a predominantly Etonian background, remembering that Eton was the fountainhead of classical Orthodoxy. Yet the heads are not erect, the backs are not held straight and the blades are no doubt about to be rowed into the water.

Another cause of the decline of Orthodoxy has been a change in the line of thought regarding the relative importance of the swing and the slide. When slides were first introduced they were regarded mainly as an extension of the swing, and when Orthodoxy was in its heyday sliding and swinging were considered of equal importance. Over the years the length of slide has steadily increased from about 9-in. up to 22-in. movement and this inevitably has caused a reduction in the swing until it has become of relatively minor importance. Where the long slide has been coupled with a pronounced swing as, for instance, in the L.M.B.C. crews of 1950–54, the efficiency of the stroke has become so high as to make it frequently impossible to raise the rate above 30 strokes per minute. It is highly doubtful whether this extreme end of the efficiency-economy scale has been justified.

It is acknowledged that the legs have the strongest muscles and it seems very logical to call upon them in preference to the stomach and back muscles to do the bulk of the work, and with the forced reduction in the swing much of the basis of Orthodoxy has been lost.

Some day a crew may appear similar to the great Orthodox crews of the past (except in that they will use swivel rowlocks): a crew of perfectly proportioned men who are strong and well-drilled enough to combine faultless bodywork and perfect bladework, and they will be a crew to watch. Personally, I think we shall have a long time to wait.

Fairbairn

As I have already mentioned the Fairbairn style originated, and gained much of its momentum, from the natural reaction against the rigid concepts of Orthodoxy. Oarsmen appeared who were unable to produce perfect body form yet whose strength and determination were perhaps greater than those who could. Rather than be classed as second-rate in Orthodox circles, they rebelled and rallied to the banner of Steve Fairbairn—the prophet of 'natural action'.

More, however, is needed to account for the many successes of Fairbairn crews and much of the credit must go to Steve Fairbairn himself. Any doctrine that is to succeed must have its prophet and the successful spread of that doctrine will depend to a considerable extent on his personality. That Steve Fairbairn had an extremely dominant personality anyone who reads his books will readily understand. It used to be said that even his presence on the towpath was sufficient to electrify all the crews on the river. In point of fact he was probably more of a trainer than a coach in the technical sense of the word, and he had that inspiring personality that is vital for any trainer if he is going to give his crew the confidence to work really hard. If one could have compared him with Hiram Conibear of the United States, and Frank Read of Canada, one would probably have found a great similarity between them.

Fairbairn's approach to rowing was a little more realistic than that of the Orthodox coaches though he always avowed that his end product was the same. Instead of demanding perfection in body movement he transferred the oarsman's attention to the other end of the oar and demanded perfection in bladework; since it is the blade in the water that moves the boat this method paid off handsomely: his crews were ready to race in less than half the time compared with Orthodox crews, since the latter spent so much time paying detailed attention to perfection of body movement as well. Not unnaturally, this led to some very odd-looking crews, where each oarsman laid most emphasis on that particular set of muscles which was best developed in him. The legs, being generally the strongest, were called upon to do most of the work and, particularly with the development of the longer slide, the swing tended to be neglected.

Whereas the greater part of Orthodox coaching was directed to increasing the efficiency of the rowing, much of Fairbairn's coaching was directed to improving the economy of effort of his crews, and his writing frequently contains such phrases as 'loose and easy', 'unscrew the tension nut', and 'if you can't do it easily you can't do it at all'—this latter is probably the most misconstrued statement ever made by a coach.

There is no doubt that under Fairbairn many oarsmen learnt to enjoy their rowing as never before; gone were the continual do's and don'ts of doctrinaire coaches, and in their place was plenty of mileage and racing with perfection of bladework as the only aim.

In the early stages of rowing the importance of the leg drive, coupled with lack of physical co-ordination, produced a blade rowed into the water with a consequential loss of length, but, as Fairbairn himself maintained, the objective was to time the spring to catch the water nearer and nearer to 'dead-centre'. Many crews never really appreciated this and were content to go banging away at the water for the rest of their lives under the impression that if they could get a 'bell-note' with the blade on the beginning then they were rowing well.

Because this method throws so little strain on the body it is possible to keep going for miles without flagging, and if the strength and stamina built up in this way are used to good purpose to get more effective length and power through the water then all is well. However, often this is not so, and today the exaggerations practised in this direction have earned almost as much opprobrium as Orthodoxy did thirty years ago.

Steve Fairbairn used to say that a good Fairbairn oarsman came in the end to row in much the same way as a good Orthodox oarsman, and this was so, inasmuch that after a period of 'natural-action' rowing the weaker muscle groups became sufficiently well developed to allow a reasonable swing and draw to be added to the leg drive, whilst perfected timing enabled the blade to grasp the water nearer and nearer to full reach.

Of all the styles, Fairbairnism is probably the most commonly practised today. It is true to say that nearly all the Continental, British and Australian crews row in this way, and remembering that no style will survive without success this is probably the finest recommendation for it of all.

Conibear

The origin of the Conibear style, like that of the Fairbairn style, is a matter of some controversy. Some say that the American style, or something very like it, was practised as long ago as 1880, others prefer the legend that Hiram Conibear, who was appointed coach to Washington University, having never touched an oar in his life, worked out a new technique from scratch with the aid of George Pocock, a boatbuilder who had emigrated from Eton and settled in Seattle.

At all events it seems likely that, like Fairbairn, Conibear was an enthusiast who inspired a remarkable improvement in the standard at Washington, and that he and his successors developed and adapted the existing American style to that which we know today.

Certainly Washington had sufficient success to attract everyone's attention to the new ideas and it is said that at one time every major American rowing university had a coach who had himself come under Conibear at Washington University; while Steve Fairbairn could have claimed much the same over here.

Arguments have raged for years over the exact interpretation of the Conibear style, and many coaches have denied its existence altogether, making the unconvincing statement that the best American crews row in a way similar to the great Orthodox crews of the past. In fact they could hardly be more different in every respect, as I hope to show.

I will now quote from an American, Robert F. Herrick, writing in *Red Top*: *the history of Harvard Rowing*. Describing the changes in style and method brought about by Tom Bolles, one of the protagonists of the Conibear style, appointed Harvard coach in 1937, he writes on page 129:

The new staff immediately started teaching the Washington style which has been so successful on the west coast in producing Olympic and Poughkeepsie winners. This consists essentially of a stroke calculated to expend the maximum energy in moving the boat forward with the least possible sousing, pinching and checking. The reach is slightly shortened and the lay-back definitely so.

The arms are broken rather early together with a sharp leg drive which blends in with a smooth draw through to a strong finish with the back only a little behind the upright position. In practice the long paddles at 18 or 20 strokes per minute are eliminated. The crews get used to paddling comfortably at 27 or thereabouts for miles on end with the result that the change to the racing pace of 31 or 32 is but a slight one not involving any major alteration in timing.

And again on page 173:

The chief differences between Washington and eastern rowing at that time were Washington's lack of lay-back, fast hands on the release and their tremendous emphasis of the catch.

From the available evidence it seems likely that the eastern style referred to was something similar to the English style. (Up till this time some American universities relied on English coaches.) The changes described by Herrick are, to some extent, a measure of the difference between Conibear and Orthodox and answer those who claim them to be identical.

It is hard to dissociate the American style from the development of the rig used and the methods of selection and training customarily employed. Basically, the changes spring from an acceptance that the leg muscles are generally strongest and should be called upon to do most of the work; this involves the use of very long slides and, inevitably, the slide coming through the work[1] and the reduction of the swing. If this can be taken for granted now I shall discuss it more fully later in the chapter.

American oarsmen are initially selected for their build and the preference is for tall men, fairly broad across the shoulders but fined down across the hips and flanks, and generally about thirteen stone—what is known as the greyhound type. Such men have a very long natural reach which, coupled with the slide coming through the work, enables them to catch the water a long way behind the rigger without strain.

Discussing the beginning earlier I said that the amount of slip can be calculated from the speed of the boat and the time taken to cover the blade, but this is not entirely true. Theoretically, it is only perfectly true if the blade enters the water with the oar at right angles to the rigger, because in any other position the oar is actually moving in the horizontal plane at an angle to the direction of flow. Perhaps it is easier to understand this by going to the other extreme: supposing an oarsman had such a long reach that he could actually bring his oar parallel to the boat at the beginning. (*See* drawing over page.)

In this position he could take a clean beginning by dropping his oar into the water as slowly as he liked without having to row an inch horizontally; this is because the water is flowing axially along the blade. Even assuming an oarsman could reach so far, to exert any pressure with the oar in this position would not move the boat forward since the pressure would be directed at right angles to the saxboard—what is generally known as 'pinching the boat'.

Allowing that this is a hypothetical case it can be seen that the nearer one approaches to it, the slower the water is moving relative to the direction of thrust of the oar, and the easier it is,

[1] i.e. The front of the seat coming aft of the thole-pin.

therefore, to catch hold of the water on the beginning. The long reach of American crews enables them to catch the water well behind the rigger without being particularly quick.

Perhaps the biggest difference between the equipment used by English and American crews is in the oars. Those used by the Americans are short inboard (3 ft. 7 in.) allowing considerable length behind the rigger, with wide blades

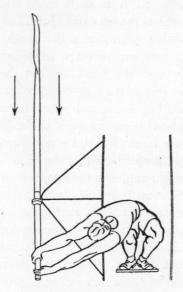

Oar parallel to the boat

(6¾ in.–7 in.), and they are deliberately made with a larger degree of flexibility than English oars. To some extent this whip in the oar acts as a cushion on the beginning and makes what might otherwise be an intolerably efficient one more comfortable. As Herrick says: the emphasis is on the 'catch'; as soon as the blade is covered tremendous pressure is applied, and the oar bends until as it approaches the most mechanically efficient position—at right angles to the saxboard—the oar is fully bent and all the pressure goes into moving the boat. The

PLATE VI

TWO GOOD FAIRBAIRN CREWS

Thames R.C. beating London R.C. in the final of the Grand Challenge Cup, 1927

PLATE VII

FAIRBAIRN

Jesus College, Cambridge, winners of the Grand Challenge Cup, 1947

PLATE VIII

CONIBEAR

Canada practising for the Empire Games on Lake Padarn, 1958. 'The arms are broken early.' (page 54)

PLATE IX

CONIBEAR

Cornell University, winners of the Grand Challenge Cup, 1957. '... finish with the back only a little behind the upright position.' (page 54)

PLATE X

RUSSIAN

Krylia Sovetov, winners of the Grand Challenge Cup, 1954. '. . . at the actual instance of the catch the blade is travelling almost vertically downwards.' (page 60)

PLATE XI

RUSSIAN

Krylia Sovetov, 1954

'. . . sit and take a rest in the most comfortable position.' (page 60)

PLATE XII

R.A.F. VIII beating Princeton University, U.S.A., in the Thames Cup. Henley Royal Regatta, 1953

'. . we scraped home a third of a length ahead.' (p. 106)

PLATE XIII

Barn Cottage, stroked by the author, beating Washington University, U.S.A., in the Stewards' Cup at Henley Royal Regatta, 1958

short inboard oar enables greater length for less reach on the beginning, and a more direct pull in the middle of the stroke, but it does not make for a long and easy finish as the end of the handle tends to land up in the middle of the chest and the outside wrist to become restricted at the finish.

The finish is made a good deal easier by the whip of the oar. What appears to happen is that as the oarsman approaches the end of the stroke he can take more time over extracting the blade, leaving the bend in the oar, as it were, to finish the stroke for him. It is as if he uses up energy on the beginning to bend the oar and then makes use of that energy to row out the finish.

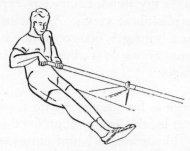

A short inboard oar

To elaborate further, if we imagine the oar to be a rigid rod, the English stroke demands a powerful finish so that an air space is created behind the blade allowing it to be extracted without the water striking the back. To effect this perfectly requires the horizontal draw to be maintained until the last instant and then to be suddenly changed for the rapid downward thrust that carries the oar out cleanly. If, on the other hand, the oar is whippy and is fully bent as it approaches the finish the oarsman can actually stop pulling the handle in towards his chest and start dropping his hands for the finish while the bend in the oar straightens out and the blade continues to push against the water.

Both beginning and finish of the American stroke make it

rather easier for the unskilled oarsman than for his English counterpart: he can be slow on the beginning and yet still catch the water well behind the rigger; he can be slow at the finish and still get his blade out cleanly. On the other hand, the average American crew does not come forward in the easiest way. The rapid thrust away of the hands, followed almost at once by the slide leaving the backstop, must use up more energy than an even-paced forward swing. In addition, the very slow sliding up to frontstops means a restriction to the lungs and a pause in a position where the leg muscles are under strain.

No one has, to my mind, completely explained the rapid hands away of Conibear crews; Americans themselves are uncertain of the advantages, one contenting himself by saying that 'all the fastest crews do it', but as I see it there are three possible advantages:

1. Since twice as long is spent with the blade out of the water as in, the best position for the boat to 'run' is clearly important. It is not unreasonable to suppose that a boat runs better with the bows high in the water and that means the oarsman's weight should be transferred to the stern of the boat as soon as possible. Hence the American cry of 'get out of bow!'

2. A shell moving through the water actually seesaws as well as moving forward, the seesaw action absorbing some of the speed of the boat and sending out little shock waves. This may be inhibited by an uneven forward movement with relatively more time spent at one end of the seesaw. (This can be easily understood by anyone who has stood with one foot on either side of a seesaw: the best way to build up the oscillations is to move the weight evenly backwards and forwards.)

3. Under stress during a race what often causes loss of pace is lack of time both to row a full-length stroke and

to poise over the stretcher, the movements slowing down due to tiredness. By always training with a rapid finish and throw away of the hands an American crew is drilled never to waste time sitting at the finish and is therefore more likely to gather over the stretcher however tired it gets.

In conclusion I will admit that my own personal preference is for the Conibear style, although I only rowed in one crew that practised on these lines—the 1953 R.A.F. VIII. However, when this crew was travelling really well there was a sizzle at the finish and a sensation of run which I have rarely experienced in any other crew.

Russian

The first Russian crews to appear in international competition since the war, namely those of 1952 and 1953, rowed in a way that differed very little from the normal continental style: they rowed an essentially Fairbairn stroke with a very relaxed forward swing and the rather high feather and early squaring that typified, for example, French and Italian crews.

In 1954 the Krylia Sovetov crews that came to Henley were somewhat different and it was clear that a new style was developing; this has become progressively more and more different from the western continental style and has influenced to a greater or lesser degree most of the eastern European countries.

In many ways the Russian style is the antithesis of Conibear, and the remarkable successes of both methods only emphasize the absurdity of a lot of the dogmatic opinions current in this country.

The efficiency of the stroke lies in the tremendous power through the water which is assisted by a remarkable beat on the beginning. The catch calls for perfect muscular co-ordination and timing; it is taken initially with the arms as rapid changes in direction and speed are most easily performed in this way. Unlike the Conibear method any slowness is fatal, and the blade is carried high on the feather, travelling round a large arc into the water. Very little length is lost at the beginning through the blade being rowed into the water, and photographs show that at the actual instant of the catch the blade is travelling almost vertically downwards. (*See* Plate X, between pages 56–7.) The way in which the vertical momentum is changed into a horizontal thrust is an indication of the amount of practise undertaken by these crews.

The finish is upright and, owing to the power of the stroke through the water, is achieved without difficulty. As the hands move away over the thighs there is a pause; unlike American crews the Russians say that they prefer to sit and take a rest when they are in the most comfortable position, which is the normal 'easy-all' position. Differing from all other styles, there is a clear-cut end to every stroke and there is no continuous chain movement. The stroke begins with the slide coming forward quite fast, the arms still bent until, just as the slide reaches the frontstop, the arms straighten and the blade circles high and latches on to the water. To row in this way requires complete relaxation without which it would be impossible to move fast enough. To beat at the water on the beginning without losing length forward and without plunging the blade in too deep calls for perfect muscular control and timing, and the high efficiency involved in the powerful thrust through the water calls for severe physical conditioning. On the other hand, the complete relaxation, together with a deliberate pause after the finish, allow a rapid change of pace during a race—the spurting powers of a good Russian crew are considerable. (In this respect it is similar to Conibear where in an emergency the pause on the frontstops can be cut down to put in a spurt.) One of the chief disadvantages of the system appears to be the rapid approach to the frontstop which has the effect of dipping the stern and using up energy in creating stern-waves. This is particularly noticeable in some of the Russian pairs and fours but, paradoxically, it is in the small-boat events that they are most successful. The Russian explanation of the theory of the bound up to frontstops is simply that of the bouncing ball: the faster the approach to frontstops the faster the rebound. In contrast to Conibear, the Russian style will not tolerate slowness or clumsiness and it is probable that it calls for more practise and is less easily taught for this reason.

Selection of Russian crews, like that of American, is an indication of their style; Russian oarsmen are impressive for their suppleness and athletic build—one feels they would be capable of succeeding in almost any sport. In this connection one noteworthy incident occurred in 1954: in the week after Henley the Russian VIII were still in this country and they obtained permission to borrow a single sculler from Leander Club. One after another they went out in her and it was significant that in spite of its being a strange boat and their being short of sculling practice, each man sculled cleanly and neatly away from the stage, blades clear of the water on the way forward, and without any unsteadiness. It was obvious that they were experienced scullers and very good watermen, and it subsequently transpired that many of them had competed successfully as scullers before they rowed in the VIII. This points a difference between eastern and western methods of selection—few American oarsmen have ever been in a sculling boat at all!

Rig

In talking about Conibear I said that a long slide means that it should come through the work and I am going to try and explain why. Going back to considering the oar as a lever of the second order, which is essentially what it is, the force of the oar on the boat always acts at right angles to the loom so that the oar is only really shoving the boat 100 per cent forward when it is at right angles to it. As the angle between oar and boat decreases some pressure is absorbed by the rigger, pushing the saxboard in or pulling it out, and this is counteracted by the oars on the other side of the boat and so wasted. As I mentioned earlier, if the oar were parallel to the boat it would not move it forward at all.

Clearly, if one intends to row the oar through, say, a sixty-degree-arc then it pays to split this up and row, effectively, thirty degrees on either side of the right-angle position,

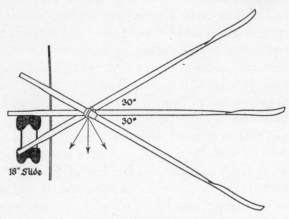

18-inch slide sliding level

assuming that equal thrust is developed throughout the stroke. In this way the minimum effort is wasted in pinching or stretching the boat.

Assume now that an oarsman on a normal 18-in. travel slide, sliding level with the work, starts using one with 22-in. movement: if he still slides up to his work he must bring his stretcher four inches nearer to him to reach his new backstop, and since he still reaches to (say) his toes, the result is something like the diagram shown on p. 63.

It will be seen that his oar is only twenty-five degrees behind the right angle on the beginning and is thirty-five degrees past

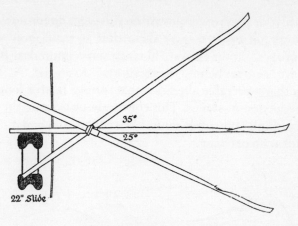

22-inch slide sliding level

it at the finish, which is wasteful. To bring his arc back to thirty degrees either side it is necessary to bring his slide-bed four inches nearer to the stern of the boat and, in fact, to slide through the work.

The cases shown are, of course, exaggerated and no one is ever likely to slide four inches through their work, nor is it

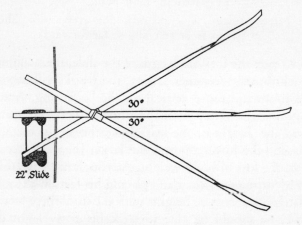

22-inch slide sliding through the work

necessarily ideal to row exactly thirty degrees either side of the right angle; in order to give them time to catch hold of the water properly most crews will reach out a good deal further than thirty degrees behind the rigger.

Another noticeable alteration that springs from a long slide is the reduction of swing. This comes about because the angle between thigh and trunk cannot be reduced beyond a certain point for each oarsman.

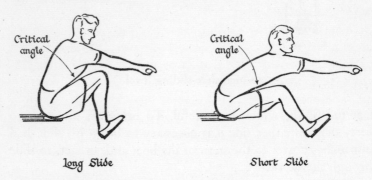

long Slide   Short Slide

The man on the left is sliding through his work. The one on the right is stopped well back. Yet both are actually reaching to exactly the same point.
(This partly explains why old orthodox crews using short slides appear to be reaching so far forward)

If one increases the forward length of the slide, maintaining the same backstop and stretcher setting, the trunk will inevitably become more and more vertical on the beginning. Actually, the critical angle varies with the distance between seat and heels and the height of the seat above the heels: the longer the slide and the lower the seat the larger the angle becomes, owing to the loss of body weight. Anyone can prove this for himself by sitting on a chair and placing his feet on a stool that is at relatively the correct height: with the stool three feet from the chair, he should be able to pack his body right down between his knees, whereas when the stool is only one foot away, or is raised up nearly level with the chair, he will be lucky to touch his knees with his shoulders.

There are, however, other factors to be considered when deciding the height of the seat relative to the heels. The higher the seat the easier it is to reach forward and, for a person of normal build, the further forward it is possible to swing; on the other hand, since, during the stroke, the only opposing horizontal forces are the pull on the handle and the drive against the stretcher, the more directly opposite these two forces are the better.

When an oarsman is taking the stroke there are a number of forces acting on him. These are: the horizontal pressure on the oar handle; the slantwise thrust from the stretcher; his weight, which acts downwards; and the residual pressure from his seat which acts upwards. All these forces, when resolved, must cancel out.

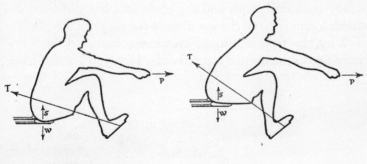

low Seat   High Seat

Showing how the angle of thrust (T) alters with height of the seat above the heels. The oarsman on the right is reaching a good deal further forward than the one on the left without any extra effort. But he is in danger of coming off his seat when he takes the stroke

The angle of thrust from the stretcher, T, is influenced by the height of the seat above the feet. If the seat is at the same level as the stretcher, T will become nearly horizontal, S, the pressure of the seat, will balance W, his weight, and nearly all his drive from the stretcher will go into pulling the oar (P). Conversely, if the seat is very much above the heels the thrust from the stretcher will tend to lift the oarsman off his seat rather than push the boat forward. This can be dangerous as well as inefficient.

The theoretical ideal is for the height of the seat to be adjusted to suit the individual oarsman, but this is not often practicable and usually the only concession that is made is to pack up the seat of an oarsman who, through lack of natural reach, is short forward. In most cases S becomes very small because the height of seat above heels is so arranged that the vertical component of T exactly counterbalances the downward force of W. But if an oarsman persists in coming off his seat when he is rowing then the answer is to lower his seat or raise his heels.

The relative inboard and outboard lengths of the oar have already been dealt with and the blade area has also been discussed. There remains the question of the shape of the blade.

Why, in fact, do some crews use barrelled blades in preference to the normal tapered ones? Firstly, it is easier to get

Barrel Blade

Taper Blade

Slightly quicker grip with
a barrelled blade

a grip on the water at the beginning with a barrel blade on account of the oar's angle of declination bringing the lower edge of the blade roughly parallel to the surface of the water. This results in a slightly smaller vertical movement being required to cover the spoon, assuming that each is poised not quite touching the water. In the second place, the barrelled blade, of similar area and weight, is a shade more efficient at holding the water. If one considers the normal tapered blade, the part of it which grips the water best is not right at the tip, because some water will spill round the end as well as round the sides—the maximum grip occurs at a point some six inches back from the end. Consequently, it seems logical to have the broadest part of the blade at the point of maximum grip.

3

Training

Why train?

TRAINING is the conditioning of mind and body for racing by repeated practice in the boat and careful regulation of life out of it. There is no sport or game which does not demand some measure of training to achieve success, and the very old saying that practice makes perfect probably applies more to rowing than to any other sport. In many games such as tennis, boxing, football, etc., one's movements depend very much on one's opponents, and what one plans and practises during training may not be of much use when it comes to the event. Rowing, on the other hand, does not rely on opposition and it is possible, though undesirable, to develop a crew from scratch and bring it up to race and win without ever seeing another crew. Moreover, as rowing is the ultimate team sport the blending of a crew to row as a unit demands more practice than would be required in the other basic sports such as running, swimming or cycling.

But training is designed to do more than achieve cohesion in a crew: it is going to develop the three S's outlined previously; in addition, the oarsman's mental discipline should develop, his watermanship improve and his confidence in his own ability increase. One might almost say that rowing *is* training.

It is surprising that, since rowing is possessed of so many people who purport to be coaches, there are so few who consider themselves trainers. Most coaches believe that their job consists in cycling or riding with their crews, correcting their technical faults and exhorting them to greater efforts when they row. Surprisingly few seem to have any idea that, unless a crew also has a trainer to set the work (which is rare), they should by rights be taking as big an interest in all the other aspects of training. My experience has been that coaches get very excited about points of style; they will argue for hours about such things as whether the beginning is the beginning of the finish or whether the finish is the beginning of the beginning; some will argue that the beginning should be a hit, others that it should be a drop, while yet others wax eloquent on the arching of the inside wrist or the virtues of holding the chin up at the finish. Yet few of them have strong views on such important matters as whether an outing should be six or twelve miles, how many minutes' rowing should be included and how early a crew should start doing full-course trials. While not denying the importance of points of style the latter questions are likely to be more important to the ultimate success of a crew.

Incredible though it may seem the work to be tackled during the outing is often left to the momentary whim of the coach, or, as is the case in many of the larger clubs, is dictated by tradition. So in the winter one finds that on Sunday mornings the crew will row a practice Head course—not because that is necessarily what is needed but because they always do. This second method is certainly the better of the two since some coaches are apt to give crews less work than they need under the impression that they are being kind, and traditional training does at least ensure a certain amount of work is done. The disadvantages of the traditional outing are, however, equally obvious. No crew has to my knowledge been made to row two Head of the River courses on a Sunday morning, however much they needed it, and crews still attempt their normal outing on the tideway when winds, rough water, tugs and yachts ensure that it will not do them a hap'orth of good. It also means that a crew is never likely to show much improvement over the crews that have gone before.

I would like to see rowing men in general, and coaches in particular, think far more about all the various aspects of training other than the increase in skill: is stamina going to be developed more by short, hard outings or by longer, steadier ones? How much work can a crew take? How much should it take? What work should be attempted on the tank? Is weight training desirable? When oarsmen and coaches start thinking seriously about these things I will know that the standard of rowing is about to go up.

Training is a personal thing

I believe that training should be a personal thing—that the basic responsibility for an oarsman's strength and fitness should lie with the oarsman himself. After all, the man does not generally come under the direct influence of coach or captain for more than two hours a day and for the other twenty-two he must use his own intelligence.

In contrast to the majority of rowing correspondents I have always credited the speed of a scullers' VIII mainly to the fact that a sculler has only himself to think about and therefore tends to take a greater interest in his own personal strength and fitness than the average crewman. The high finishing position of the London Scullers' VIII in the Head of the River in recent years has not been due to better watermanship nor to some mystical ability with an oar that can only be acquired by sculling, but to the fact that individually the crew was a good deal fitter than the great majority of those they were competing against. The man who takes up rowing seriously should not leave it to his club to make him train, but should take every step within his power to improve his own performance in the boat, and to this end he should consider himself in training for twenty-four hours a day.

There are three basic functions necessary to rowing: exercise, relaxation and eating, and every single minute of the day should be classified accordingly in the light of the requirements of rowing. The first-class oarsman will always be thinking about his rowing. He will eat with a view to replacing energy used up and to building tissue. Whatever he does during the day, while he is at work, exercise for rowing and relaxation for rowing should be at the back of his mind. If he has to sit he should try and relax completely; if he has to walk about he should do so briskly, remembering that walking is excellent out-of-the-boat training. Sedentary and office workers should try and get some exercise in the fresh air as often as possible, for instance during the lunch hour, striding along and breathing deeply. Manual workers should avoid cramped positions and should try and relax for a few minutes whenever the opportunity arises.

One thing that stood out among the early R.A.F. crews was the intensely personal attitude to training developed at Benson and which is illustrated by a true story. In November 1953 we were working on the new R.A.F. Rowing Club and one of the crew, Ted Field, having finished work at 5 p.m., went straight down to the club and laid drain-pipes until 10 p.m. He then returned to camp, had his supper and, feeling tired, went to bed. At 11.30 p.m. the rest of his billet were awakened to see him getting dressed in his running-kit and departing into the night. Enquiries the next morning elicited the fact that as he had not done his normal training his conscience would not let him sleep and he had got up and gone for a five-mile run. This approach to training was typical of many of these oarsmen.

The development of such an attitude in a club is not difficult and is most easily effected by competition between individual members. When the crew goes running, every man struggles to beat the rest and the last man receives the jibes. After a little of this, if he has any guts, he will probably be found putting in some extra practice on his own.

At Benson everyone was called upon to race in a pair of matched rum-tums down to Cleeve Lock and back—a distance of 10½ miles—and times varied from the 1 hr. 26 min. of the fastest to the most recently arrived oarsman who was thrust into a sculling boat for the first time in his life and told to get on with it. He took a little under three hours. Nor was it unknown for two of the crew, who had been having a difference of opinion, to get into a pair from which the rudder had been removed and, starting on our straight stretch, to row until the boat hit the bank one side or the other.

Winter and summer

Every so often that hardy perennial pops up—'should one train in the boat during the winter?' or even, 'should one train at all during the winter?' It is sometimes said that rigorous training throughout the winter in miserable conditions is more likely to make a crew sick of rowing than to do them any good, and that they would be better off confining their winter training to light exercise ashore or occasional outings in a tub pair to brush up their technique. In this way, it is argued, they would return to rowing in the spring, fresh and invigorated and yearning to buckle down to training again.

Let me say at once I am wholly and completely on the side of those who demand all-the-year-round training, with perhaps a short break in the autumn. If one looks at the other sports which demand stamina and technique and which are more highly developed than rowing there are few which call for a long break during the year; not many first-class athletes could afford to take a rest in the winter and top-class tennis players, swimmers and cyclists train all the year round. 'Practice makes perfect' as much in rowing as in other spheres, and generally the more practice the nearer perfect.

One amateur tennis champion is said to have practised

when he was young by hitting a tennis ball up against a wall for five hours every day: this strengthened his wrist and aided his eyesight and judgement of pace and undoubtedly helped him to beat the rest of the world. Reg Harris, several times professional world sprint cycling champion, spent some five hours a day in the saddle apart from strengthening exercises in the gymnasium. Zatopek, outstanding athlete of our time, would run thirty miles a day throughout the year. Nor is rowing short of examples of men who have trained as rigorously and reaped a rich harvest.

Given that training throughout the winter is essential I will go further and say that training in the boat as often as possible is desirable. I have spent four successive winters rowing several nights a week in the dark and my unqualified advice to any oarsman or crew wishing to succeed is to do likewise. Rowing from Putney I have gone out on a Saturday afternoon in the winter when there have been rough water, yachts going in all directions, tugs with barges, crews coxed or steered by idiots crossing above bridges or travelling in the centre of the river against the tide, driftwood and sundry other hazards. I have also gone afloat after dark during the week when I could have read a newspaper standing on the Putney hard, there have been no yachts, no other crews, seldom any tugs, the water has been smooth and clear reflecting the lights from the bridges and embankments—yet it is said that boating after dark is dangerous! In all the many miles (well over 1,500) that I have rowed after dark, only once have I ever known a mishap and that was when we were out in a coxless IV and our bow and steers took us through the inside arch of Hammersmith Bridge on a rather low tide: the skin touched the ground and we had to bale out.

Looking back I think I can honestly say I have preferred evening rows in the winter to those undertaken during the daytime.

If a crew is going to boat after dark one essential is that it should carry a light in the bows to be seen by, for although the ordinary bicycle lamp will not show the way it can be seen clearly from quite a distance. Those who have experience of driving down quiet country roads will know how much safer it is by night than during the day owing to the visibility of approaching headlights. So it is on the river: one can glance over one's shoulder in the daylight and miss the occasional sculler or crew, but I defy anyone not to see an oncoming torchlight shining from the even darkness of the river at night.

Colleges and schools can of course boat during daylight hours in the week so that this does not apply so much to them, but clubs that are restricted to weekend daylight outings have to decide whether they are going to row several nights a week throughout the winter or make do with two outings at the weekends. My experience of weekend rowing, unsupported by other training, is that much of it is unproductive. Unless the members of the crew have been active in the week it takes them most of the Saturday outing to get used to the boat and crew again and, owing to loss of fitness, they are frequently too tired to do much good work on the Sunday.

There are oarsmen who can get by without continuous rowing throughout the winter and one may cite Leadley and Davidge, winners of the European Championship pairs in 1957, who did not get down to really serious training until February of that year. But both these oarsmen are possessed of great natural strength and both have done many years of continuous and hard winter rowing at college so that their reserves of stamina are considerable. To hold back from training till the spring is a very dangerous experiment which certainly no oarsman of normal standard can afford to make. Those crews who have started late can often be seen racing at their best at the last regatta of the season, by which time regular racing every Saturday throughout the summer has sufficed to make them fit; but by then the very reason for training no longer exists.

Fitness is a much abused word which really has no specific meaning. 'Of course I believe in getting the crew fit' one coach will say; yet there are many standards of fitness. One can be fit to row twenty miles at 22 strokes to the minute and not be fit to row four miles at 28. The crew that can cover the Head of the River course at 30 could blow up in a one-mile race attempting to row at 33. Similarly, a crew that is fit enough to row 44 strokes in a minute may not have the stamina to row at 34 for three minutes.

Winter is the ideal time to build up stamina; the weather is cold enough to allow plenty of long-distance rowing without fining the crew down too much, and it is usually too chilly to permit them to sit about practising the nicer points of technique. Long-distance rowing at a good driving rate of 24–30 covering anything from three to six miles at a stretch, with a total of anything between ten and fifteen miles, is a reasonable target. In the winter three or four night outings of six or eight miles coupled with long weekend rows are ideal, but many crews will have to settle for one or two if the members live at a distance from the club. If this is the case a couple of out-of-the-boat training nights a week in addition will go a long way to make up the deficiency.

I have always found a mileage chart a great help to winter training. This consists of a sheet of graph paper with total miles plotted up the vertical axis and time in weeks along the horizontal. At the beginning of training a target line of so many miles per week is drawn on to the chart. At the end of each week the total mileage is plotted and the crew can follow their progress compared with their target. Below is the winter mileage chart I kept for the R.A.F. crews in 1953 and 1954. It will be seen that with the lighter evenings the target increased and that it was set high enough to make it difficult for us to achieve.

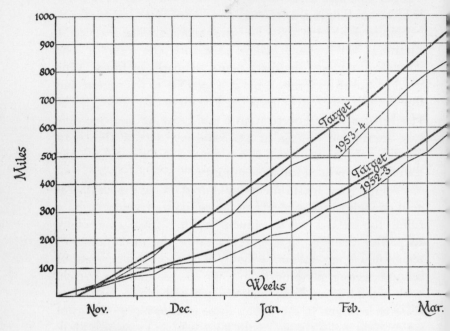

Winter mileage chart. R.A.F. VIIIs 1953 and 1954

April and May are the two most important months in the year as the foundation of successful summer racing is built during this period. Yet April at least is often one of the slackest months when it should be one of the busiest on the river. The light evenings should see the crews getting down to training on the water at least five times a week. Strength and basic stamina-building should largely be completed and the emphasis laid on instilling racing stamina and the development and retention of technique under stress.

One of our creeds in the R.A.F. was that Henley races are won before the beginning of June, and every crew that rowed for the R.A.F. in those days was ready to race long before this.

During April and May crews should aim at an average of ten miles an outing, depending upon how much work is undertaken. In any case a flat-out row of at least one mile (or six minutes) should be done each day, but with the warmer weather the work can be split up to include alternate bursts of rowing and paddling, repetitive rowing and interval rowing, all of which help to develop that all-important racing stamina.

I believe that out-of-the-boat training is less desirable during the summer months and that the whole attention of the crew should be directed towards rowing. If one feels an urge to take any additional exercise out of the boat the rowing should be increased until the urge disappears!

The indoor tank

Of all out-of-the-boat training the indoor tank (or the bank tub) is the most useful in that it is the only commonly available form of exercise which is designed to reproduce ashore the effect of rowing. In the winter the tank is used (some would say abused) a great deal, for neither frost nor fog, gales nor darkness will hinder its use.

To me the tank has two purposes. It should be used by all novices to learn the basic movements of oar control before being allowed near a boat; there they can sit for hours on end, feeling the balance of an oar and learning the tricks of squaring and feathering and how to take hold of the beginning and roll the oar away at the finish. When an oarsman is reasonably proficient the tank becomes so unlike a racing boat that it is pointless to practise technique in it and the tank then becomes a machine to aid physical development. I believe the tank should be used to build up strength and stamina and this can only be done by sitting down and rowing as hard as possible for, say, fifteen minutes; after this time the muscles, particularly those of the back and arms, become tired enough for muscle development to begin, moreover it is impossible to build up useless muscles since none are brought into play which are not used in rowing. But the muscles are not necessarily built up in relatively the correct proportions. For instance, in a boat the beginning is heavy and as the shell gathers speed so the work becomes faster and lighter; the reverse is the case in the tank where the oar is wholly a lever of the first order relying entirely on slip. Because of this the blade is perforated and so slips quite easily on the beginning; however, owing to a build up of water at the aft end of the tank, and the slip being reduced, the stroke becomes progressively harder as it nears the finish. What tends to happen is that the muscles used in the 'draw'—arms and back—are developed to a greater extent than, for instance, the legs, which are, inevitably, driven down first. Still, as most other out-of-the-boat exercises—running, skipping, etc.—concentrate on the legs, this may be no bad thing.

The main drawback to the tank, apart from that already mentioned, is its lack of flexibility. In a boat one can put in a few extra hard strokes and feel it run faster as a result; the increased momentum helps the hands to come away and the slide to leave the backstop; also, the beginning becomes lighter. No such rewards accrue from extra effort on the tank and this leads to the dull, plodding rowing that is an all too common feature of prolonged tanking.

Quickness of movement is one of the skills most required in rowing and monotonous tanking is a sure way to destroy it. Consequently, tanking should be cut down very severely in the summer months when sprint races require maximum speed. In any case it is advisable to combine tanking with other out-of-the-boat training as, for example, skipping and running, where the accent is on speed and agility rather than strength.

Too many oarsmen approach the tank as an aid to developing technique and in this I am sure they are wrong. It is true that if a coach has been unable to make a point clear he can put a man in the tank and show him his mistake, but this hardly comes under the heading of training. Otherwise, the lack of movement robs the tank of nearly all it has to offer in practising technique. It cannot be of technical value to take a beginning when the water is stationary as the theoretical blade movement should then be vertically downwards at the catch. Likewise, there should be no similar problem in getting the blade clear at the finish as there is little vacuum behind it and little water momentum to strike the back of it if the finish is slow. With no acceleration to the finish there is no natural rebound, and consequently there must be an artificial pull forward with the straps.

In spite of all these drawbacks the indoor tank can provide all the facilities for developing the muscular stamina and strength that are required for rowing, and it should therefore be the first line of support for in-the-boat training during the winter.

Callisthenics

Callisthenics are exercises for promoting gracefulness and strength, so that all exercises carried out as an aid to rowing can be classed under this heading. However, out-of-the-boat exercises can serve many different purposes and it is as well to bear in mind exactly what is required.

Any period of callisthenics should begin with loosening exercises which do not call for much physical effort, and where the aim is to get all the muscles into a warm and free condition, to get the lungs filled with fresh air and to work up a sweat. Such things as running on the spot, easy skipping, and simple exercises like trunk rolling, squats, arm swinging, etc., will all help to tone the body up and prepare it for a greater output of energy.

Exercises which are an aid to breathing include such things as skipping and running—particularly running up stairs. Another useful way of practising deep breathing is to walk very briskly and see how many steps you can take to each inhalation and how many to each exhalation. I have found this a very useful exercise to do before breakfast when one wants to fill the lungs and get on one's toes without becoming too violent or sweaty. Ten minutes' really brisk walking is all that is needed and if you can continuously take fifteen paces to each inhalation and another fifteen to each exhalation you are doing well. Of course, the faster you walk the more frequently you can breathe, but since you use up more oxygen, the quicker you need to breathe.

Skipping is useful for muscular co-ordination and in the R.A.F. we used to do a variation of 'squats' which we found good for muscle control. This exercise we used to call 'deep knee bends' and it consisted of going through the movements of sculling standing up. Stand with the heels together, feet splayed as on the stretcher, and come forward (that is, down), the hands following the imaginary arcs of a pair of sculls, trunk swinging forward and, finally, legs bending to bring up the slide. As the buttocks approach the heels so the hands (fingers loosely rolled) reach out as far either side of the feet as possible. Now take the beginning—legs thrusting upwards, trunk opening up the angle between body and thigh, hands drawing upwards at the sculls so that the muscles down the back become clenched with the effort. Finish with the body erect, shoulders rolled right back with the hands drawn into the sides as the handles of the sculls come apart again. Done with vim this exercise can be one of the most useful possible. Because no weights are involved it is impossible to strain anything and, after all, if oarsmen claim to pull their own weight in the boat it is not much to ask them to lift it up and down. Even so it is surprising how many supposedly fit oarsmen are unable to reach 200 without looking groggy.

Another leg exercise, which I believe was practised by the Japanese crew in Melbourne, 1956, consists of standing with the legs wide apart and going down on one leg, keeping the other one straight, then straightening up and going down on

Deep knee bends

the other leg. At first you will probably need to use your arms to balance with, but without putting your fingers on the ground.

The ultimate is, of course, to stand on one leg and do squats without the other one touching the ground, but this calls for a very high strength-to-weight ratio and I can only suggest that anyone who finds even this easy should do it with a weight across his shoulders.

An exercise for strengthening stomach muscles is to sit down on the floor with the feet wedged under some object (or get someone to hold them). Swing the trunk back gently till the head touches the floor, and then up and forward as far as possible without bending the knees. At first it is advisable to place the hands behind the neck; later it should be possible to carry them above the head at arm's length. A word of warning —this exercise should not be attempted more than ten times in the first try as it is very easy to strain the stomach muscles. The R.A.F. crew were once inveigled into doing it by the physical training instructors on a standard aircrew fitness test. Because full marks were only achieved by 125 bends we all did this

Go down on alternate legs

number and, as a result, we walked about bent forward for the next fortnight.

Nowadays, circuit training has come to the fore in rowing as well as in athletics: it consists of following a round of exercises (with and without weights), each performed a set number of times. The circuit may be repeated and, after a period, the work intensified either by shortening the intervals of rest, increasing the number of repetitions, using heavier weights—or by all three. Some of these circuits have been worked out for athletes in other branches of sport and some for all-round physical development and herein lies the danger. Oarsmen should not attempt to build muscles other than those used in rowing: they are useless weight in the boat and often conflict with the rowing muscles, therefore it pays to leave out all exercises for strengthening these other muscles except, possibly, the very simple loosening ones.

Too many circuit-training programmes that I have seen include such items as 'press-ups' and I fail to see how these, which bear no relation to rowing, can be of any possible value to oarsmen. Treat with suspicion remarks that oarsmen should go in for 'all-round development' and hints that men who do nothing but row will become in some way deformed. If your main interest is in rowing then do not be sidetracked into developing muscles for anything else, or, if you want to build a 'body beautiful', do not attempt to row as well—it just does not work!

Weight-training

Weight-training is in many ways like tanking, in that it is a useful way of building up muscular strength if it is properly handled. I stress *properly handled* because I think there are more pitfalls and dangers in the use of weights than with any other kind of training.

Training with weights has the obvious advantage that it does not require expensive equipment, like an indoor tank, and can even be carried out at home. Also, it is possible to bring about what is, I believe, called 'muscular saturation' (which is the condition where a muscle is unable to repeat a contraction that it has already performed a few times) more quickly than by any other method. Driving a muscle to these limits repeatedly increases its capacity.

If one is exercising a particular muscle that is used in rowing in this way it becomes stronger and so, theoretically at any rate, becomes capable of applying more power to the blade. However, an oarsman's power is only as strong as his weakest link and this is the danger of weight-training—it is very selective. When an oarsman takes a stroke the thrust is transmitted from his stretcher to the oar handle. To do this it must pass through his legs, his stomach and buttock muscles, up his back to his shoulders and finally down his arms to his wrists and fingers; only by developing all these sets of muscles to the same extent is the oarsman going to become really stronger as far as rowing is concerned. If, for example, he practises doing 'squats' with a weight across his shoulders, and also 'arm bends' with a weight in each hand, he may well find his legs shoving on the stretcher and his upper back muscles drawing well, but, because the muscles in the lower part of the trunk are not developed to the same degree, the thrust is lost between the two and the small of the back gives under the strain. This is where correct use of weights can help: if an oarsman has a weak point during the stroke, as, for instance, his back not being able to contain and transmit the drive from the legs, then weight-training can be used to strengthen that particular set of muscles.

So far as the normal oarsman is concerned I am in no way qualified to suggest a series of exercises that can be done to bring about an all-round development of the rowing muscles. To be frank, I have always fought shy of weight-training and preferred to develop strength by rowing in the boat or on the tank, but this is because I have never spoken to anyone who was fully conversant with the principles of weight-training, and who could correlate the act of rowing with all the individual muscle groups that are used. In my opinion there is a need for a really authoritative book on weight-training for oarsmen and until it appears I am not going to recommend all-round development by the use of weights. My own limited experience, which resulted in my straining my abdominal muscles, suggests that weight-lifting should be done with weights that are handled with ease, at least at the start of the exercise, rather than in a spirit of competition to see who can lift the most.

Weight-training is useful solely in building up strength; it does not do much to develop stamina and nothing at all to develop skill. Strength and speed generally work in opposition, and exercises designed to increase strength often result in slowness. For this reason it has been suggested that tanking should be reduced to a minimum in the summer, and if this applies to tanking, it applies even more to weight-training. Speed, by which I mean quickness of muscle reaction, is vital to skill and that is another of the three S's, so increasing strength alone will often reduce skill, for which reason it pays to be very cautious in one's approach to weight-training and to be certain of balancing it with exercises designed to encourage quickness.

There have been obvious cases of oarsmen and scullers who have done a great deal of weight-training and, as a result, have become strong, ponderous and slow; it must be one of life's mysteries to them that some light-weight, who hardly has the strength to carry his boat down to the water, goes haring past them in the race.

My advice to anyone who is aware of physical weakness and would like to overcome it is to approach one of the instructors at any gymnasium or institute of physical education who specializes in this subject, explain very carefully what is required, and ask him to suggest specific exercises which will strengthen those particular muscles used in rowing.

Running

As already mentioned running is an ideal toning-up exercise. However stiff or tired one might be after a day's work a relaxed trot over two or three miles, wearing plenty of warm clothing, should serve to loosen up the muscles, get the lungs breathing deeply and the blood circulating freely. In very cold weather particularly a short run is the best way to prepare for other exercises (including rowing) which call for greater output of physical strength.

Running is also very good for the wind, and for someone who has laid off training for a period, breathlessness can be one of the most painful afflictions to result from the reintroduction of violent exercise. Before rowing or serious training starts again in the winter a few quiet runs in the preceding weeks will help to stave off at least some of the anguish. Getting a lead on the other members of the crew is well worth while; as outing by outing the crew get fitter so your own fitness improves, and if you can keep one jump ahead it makes the work just that much easier. This crafty attitude was much in evidence with the R.A.F. crew. I remember one October evening some three weeks before the start of winter rowing thinking that it would be a good idea to amble gently round our three-mile circuit and get myself into a reasonable condition in advance. While I was out I met several more of the crew at various points on the road and more than half of them did not know the others were out.

Running uphill or sprinting up a long flight of steps is a wonderful exercise for reaching down deep into the lungs. At Henley in 1954, when I reckoned to be as fit as I ever was, I used to walk down a very steep pathway to the river and sprint up it as fast as I could every morning before breakfast. It served to remind me that everyone could always get a little fitter. Apart from its purely physical value running has other uses for the oarsman. For one thing it can teach him to think, and that is something oarsmen as a whole tend not to do. To go running, particularly with others, can teach an oarsman to pace himself in competition—a very desirable accomplishment. Obviously it is no use sprinting away at an uneconomical pace if one is going to suffer the indignity of being passed by the rest of the field before the finish. Generally it pays to keep to the pack for a bit, settle into an economical stride and see how things develop, then, at some critical point when things appear to be flagging, lengthen the stride and see if you can forge ahead. Some people can be broken by a sudden devastating sprint, others by a succession of short 'hardening on' periods, yet others by a steadily increasing pace.

Ideally this sort of strategic planning is best carried out in sculling boats, but all too often there are insufficient to go round or the sculling ability of the crew may vary too much. Often captains may be unwilling to sacrifice time that could be spent in the VIII. Every oarsman should be able to run with some degree of ability and running as a crew can be used to introduce that measure of guile and strategy which is possessed by every really good oarsman.

This brings us on to racing. Unless the intention of the run is to loosen up before other exercise, all running should be with the object of getting over the course as fast as possible, and, if several take part, of beating the rest. Racing spirit and the will to win should invade every single activity undertaken by the oarsman (except weight-lifting), and running is no exception. All too often one sees two or more oarsmen out for a training run, ambling along at the pace of the slowest, presumably under the impression that they are doing themselves good.

If a crew is going to do much running and some members are consistently faster than the others, it is a good idea to start on handicap so that everyone finishes together.

Finally, there is the marathon. There appears to be no logical justification for making oarsmen go on really long runs (upwards of fifteen miles), but I am a firm believer in the value of a limited number of such outings; one or two a year, well spaced from all races, are usually sufficient to serve their purpose and to tell the captain all he needs to know about his crew. The 'Henley run' (Benson airfield to Henley Bridge and back—a round trip of twenty miles) was started by our cox, who, after much ragging, set out to prove that there was something he could do better than anyone else. Once he had accomplished it, it was inevitable that everyone else should go, and the date chosen for the very first trip was immediately after the Christmas holiday when everyone was somewhat overloaded with good food. Every single oarsman on camp went, and the times varied between 2 hr. 50 min. for the fastest to 5 hr. 45 min. for the newest member, who had taken the wrong turning and gone the long way round. Naturally people were stiff afterwards but the run taught us some valuable things. It told us who had the guts to go on driving himself when the tears of weariness were running down his face—and who had let his personal training slip during the Christmas holiday!

'Going into training'

There are probably more absurd notions on 'going into training' than over anything else. I have frequently been asked what I think a crew ought to do when, as they put it, they go 'into training'—all too often for a race that is only a few weeks away.

When an oarsman undertakes to row he should immediately start to regulate his existence so that nothing conflicts directly with his rowing; as he acquires proficiency and his aspirations grow, so the amount of training he does should increase and the tighter control he should exercise over his other activities. There should be no start to a training period and no stop; whether an oarsman is spending fifteen hours a week on the water in the summer, or is taking a rest during the autumn, he is still, to a greater or lesser degree, 'in training'. To fix a date a certain number of weeks before a race, and say that then the crew will go into strict training, is largely useless, and indicates a fundamentally wrong approach on the part of the coach or captain.

There is often a misplaced emphasis on aspects of training, and if you talk to the typical oarsman about being in strict training he will most likely consider foregoing smoking, limiting his consumption of beer and getting to bed early, rather than taking so much exercise in the boat that these things become more a matter of self-preservation than a series of rules and regulations.

If you happen to smoke and can convince your captain and coach that you are rowing as powerfully and hard as if you did not, you have a good case for continuing to smoke—the fact that the great majority of top-class athletes abstain is an indication that they have failed to convince themselves that smoking is not detrimental to their performance. Similarly, if you can do all that is asked of you in the boat within an hour of eating a large helping of suet pudding, then by all means eat suet pudding. If anyone tells me that they do satisfy these conditions I shall be inclined to think that they are not being asked to do enough in the boat. The oarsman who is doing the proper sort of training, by which I mean something like two hours' hard rowing every day, will be only too anxious to get to bed early, to regulate his eating and drinking and to cut down on his other activities. When I was rowing really hard I used to sleep ten hours a night, I loathed the taste of beer, ate simply at all times and with great moderation during the four hours before an outing, and was very rude to anyone who smoked within a radius of five yards. Even so, towards the end of every outing I would resolve to do more in the future.

There are books which deal in far greater detail with what is, and what is not, desirable for an oarsman in training, so that I do not propose to expand on it now. Briefly, I do not think an oarsman should smoke, or drink more than the very occasional glass of beer or wine; he should cut down on his eating during the summer (something which is easier said than done), so that he gets up from each meal still slightly hungry. A short walk before breakfast is a good idea, at least in the summer, and the need for plenty of sleep should be self-evident. Crowded places should be avoided and he should not spend more time standing around during the day than is necessary. On the other hand I see no advantage in limiting the total amount of water drunk each day, or forbidding completely any food of which the oarsman is particularly fond, and there can be no objection to watching television or going to the occasional cinema or theatre, provided, of course, that it does not conflict with training time and that the atmosphere is not stuffy nor the seats cramped.

A sense of proportion is very necessary if one is to preserve an appetite for rowing and I have found that if the required amount of training is done in the boat there is usually little necessity for rigid controls ashore.

4

Racing

What makes for speed?

THERE was a senior R.A.F. officer who showed a good deal
of interest in the R.A.F. Rowing Club when it was first
formed in 1953, and when he suggested coming down and
coaching us we agreed eagerly. However, it rapidly became
obvious that his ideas were hardly going to be considered
seriously by us. On his first (and last) outing he set us an
eight-minute course with the injunction to row 'as long as
you can and as deep as you can and as hard as you can and
as fast as you can'. This phrase brought him immortality,
at least in the history of R.A.F. rowing, and has been used
again and again when lightheartedly speeding a crew on its
way to the start of a race.

Yet there is a lot of sense in the remark, some part of which
often gets overlooked. 'As long as you can and as deep as you
can' mean an efficient stroke with little slip, 'as hard as you
can' infers maximum power and 'as fast as you can' means at
as high a rating as can be maintained. Here are all the components for absolute pace in a boat, or if you prefer it as an
equation:

$$\text{Speed} = \text{length} \times \text{power} \times \text{rating}.$$

The validity of this expression can be seen by putting any term
on the right equal to zero.

One can increase the rating, but if it is at the expense of the length in the water the boat does not go faster; alternatively, one can shorten the stroke and row the blade through harder without losing pace; but the only way to row longer, deeper, harder and faster is to build up strength and stamina.

As a generalization one might say that, over a short period, efficiency $\times$ rating $=$ a constant, and this constant is what might be called the racing stamina of the oarsman or crew.

We had an example of this with our 1953 VIII. Having no coaching during the spring, and covering a fair amount of mileage at a high rate, we developed a rather short economical stroke and when we had a practice race against Balliol College, at that time Head of the River at Oxford, we beat them by four lengths in a five-minute row during which our rate did not fall below 39. The same day Christopher Davidge was posted to the station and started to coach us. He made us catch the beginning quicker and hold out the finishes longer; altogether he made the crew a great deal more efficient—but by Henley we could not row a mile at a higher rate than 35 and our best pace had become 33. Here was a case where our efficiency had increased at the expense of our rating and it was by no means certain by how much our overall pace had gone up.

Coaches, of course, want it both ways and the manner in which a coach will set about his task—first adding a little bit of efficiency by, say, getting the crew to hang on to the finishes, and then giving them a piece of work, or putting them alongside another crew so that they are encouraged to put the rate up a trifle—is one of the fascinations of rowing. What they are working for is to increase the efficiency $\times$ rating factor which I have called the racing stamina of the crew and on which its speed depends. There is practically no limit to the improvement of a crew if it can continue developing this factor. Greater efficiency may be promoted in a number of ways—longer strokes, less slip, more power, larger blades, etc., and the rate can be increased to the limits of the muscular contraction needed to manipulate the oar.

I keep talking about this critical factor—racing stamina, and indeed I have stated that at any time this is roughly constant and is a measure of the speed of the crew, but I have not yet really defined it: the racing stamina of an oarsman is the amount of energy he can put into moving the boat at a racing pace over the course in question.

If you imagine a car engine being designed to take part in a race of a given distance and that an exact amount of petrol is provided on which to drive it, then obviously an engine above a certain size is eliminated outright because it will use up all the petrol before the end of the race. But there still remains a choice: whether to design the engine with large cylinders and a long stroke to run at a low number of revolutions per minute and a high gear ratio, or to incorporate small cylinders designed to operate at more r.p.m. and lower gearing—each to use the same amount of petrol.

In this analogy the piston stroke is the effective length of the blade in the water and the bore is its area; the number of r.p.m. is equivalent to the rate of striking. A slightly greater speed can be brought about by tuning the engine and making certain every scrap of petrol is used to drive the car (improving the skill of the crew), but the only way to go much faster is to increase the allowance of petrol and, if you have not already guessed, the petrol allocation is symbolic of the racing stamina of the crew.

Racing stamina has been mentioned briefly in the chapter on training but I am going to deal with it more fully here as it is the essence of winning. It is increased by repeated training at a racing pitch and at the state of extreme mental and physical fatigue which one associates with a hard race.

Long-distance races

By long-distance races I mean anything over two miles or lasting more than about ten minutes. There is, of course, no fundamental difference between a race of 500 yards and one of five miles but such arbitrary divisions provide useful frames of reference. In this country we tend to think of long-distance races in the winter and spring and to include the Boat Race and the many Head of the River races. Very few long-distance races are held in the summer with the occasional exception of the Wingfield Sculls.

THE HEAD OF THE RIVER RACE

Arguments are frequently advanced denying the general desirability of racing in the early part of the season and, in particular, of setting out to win the Head of the River. It is urged that to concentrate on high ratings in the early months distracts attention from the more important job of instilling technique and paying heed to basic individual faults. I can see no justification for this attitude, believing that the whole object of rowing is to win races and that if technique cannot be perfected under racing conditions then it will seldom remain perfect under test.

The 'Head of the River' is a race, and if one enters for it one should enter with the intention of winning. The excuses produced (usually afterwards) about not wanting to bring the crew on too soon, or to distract their attention from their rowing by making them go over at a high rate, stamp the crew and the coach that are going to have little success in the following summer. An oarsman must have an insatiable appetite for winning all his races and if he has not got one the the sooner he is made to develop it the better.

As I said, the problem of learning to race over a long distance is exactly the same as for that over a short distance: namely how to maintain an effective racing gait without deterioration, and this can only be done by logical training.

The long-distance race is won by one of the usually small number of crews which prepare for the race properly and any crew, even those coming in after the one hundred mark in the Head of the River, could get up into the first ten if it set about intensive training for it.

The simplest method of winning the Head of the River is to row more full courses than anyone else, and, better still, to row a distance greater than the actual course: this is the method we used in 1954 in the R.A.F. We had a rather weak crew, including two juniors who had never even rowed in the race before, and we were determined to win the 'Head'. We set out to row 1,000 miles between mid-November and the race at the end of March; the fact that we only covered 880 was due to a long cold spell in February when the river froze solid. During this time our rate rarely dropped below 29 strokes to the minute and we rowed our boathouse-to-lock course of five and a quarter miles (average time twenty-six minutes) no less than fifty-three times, and of these twenty-two were complete 'lock to locks' over six and a half miles. For four weeks before the race we rowed a course every day six days a week, rowing the five-mile on Monday, Tuesday, Thursday and Friday evenings and the six-and-a-half-mile on Wednesday and Saturday afternoons. During these rows we would get about 34 strokes into the first minute, settle to 30 and build it up in the last mile to finish at 36 or 38. All these rows were done at full pressure against the clock, and on the journey back to the boathouse, when we were all really tired, we would have a concentrated blitz on the technique, rowing shorter stretches at 28 to 30.

This sort of training makes it difficult not to win the Head of the River—assuming no one else does the same!—and our greatest worry, when we came to the Tideway, was how we were going to sprint over the course fast enough to use up all our energy in a twenty-minute row. The race itself was practically the lightest outing we had had.

I have expatiated on the training of this 1954 R.A.F. crew because, individually, they were not outstanding oarsmen, and because they had to develop their racing stamina from scratch. The Thames R.C. VIII which won in 1955 were stronger and more experienced, so that although they trained on similar lines they did not need to row quite so many full courses. The crews which won in 1956 and 1958 were both fairly scratch, but virtually all the oarsmen in them had undergone the same stamina-building training in previous years and all were well aware of the need for race conditioning.

The 1954 crew, on the other hand, achieved its success with no better material than the average small club has to draw on and for this reason I am quoting, word for word, our training log as I recorded it, day by day, for a fortnight towards the end of February. I have made it a practice to keep a log of every outing undertaken by regular crews that I have rowed with because I believe that later they can be a valuable guide to assessing the causes of a successful or unsuccessful season, and also, because they are written at the time, they are truthful accounts of what training actually was done and what the feelings of the crew were—things that tend to become exaggerated and distorted over the years.

ACTUAL RECORD FROM THE TRAINING LOG OF THE
R.A.F. VIII, 1954

Crew:	Bow	Cranmer
	2	Arber
	3	Bickley
	4	Harrison
	5	Brasher
	6	Buchanan
	7	Kitchener
	Str.	Porter
	Cox	Staal

15.2.54 Straight down to the lock [5¼ m.] Chris [Davidge] in launch which broke down at the Pylons. Towed launch the last 2 miles on the way back, Chris sitting astride the bows, slow progress. Rowing not too bad on the way down.   10½ miles.

16.2.54 Field and Rand replaced Bickley and Harrison at 3 and 4. Rowed straight down to Cleeve [5¼ m.] and back—Pylons, home. Not bad but rather unsteady and timing not too good. Slow on the beginning.   10½ miles.

17.2.54 Rowed lock to lock [6½ m.] in 34.44. Stream subsided a lot. Not a bad time considering headwind and fairly slow conditions. Back Pylons and home. Rowed in [2 m.] in 12.47 not so good. Rating 31 and 30 both ways.   13 miles.

18.2.54 Sorrell arrived on the Station and came in at 2, Arber going out. Rowed straight down to Cleeve rating 31–30 with strong stream. Sorrell rather sick on the way down. Back in two pieces. Slow and heavy on beginnings.   10½ miles.

19.2.54 River flooded and covered with debris. No outing.

20.2.54 Rowed lock to lock with very strong stream in 30.10. Not at all good rowing. Very heavy indeed on beginning. Rand moved up to 6, Buchanan back to 4. Rowed from Cleeve to Pylons [3 m.] against the stream with Oxford and Thames R.C. crews. R.A.F. in centre (!) Close finish, T.R.C., R.A.F. and O.U.B.C. in that order.   13 miles.

21.2.54 Outing with Thames R.C. VIII. Paddled up to Benson [1 m.] and back, then rowed to Cleeve [5 m.]. Good row, crews neck and neck all the way to the Beetle and Wedge, then R.A.F. went away to win by about 3 lengths.

Very weary coming back.   13 miles.
Total mileage for week: 70½.

22.2.54 Sorrell moved from 2 to 4 and Field 3 to 2, Arber coming in at 3 and Buchanan going out. Rowed straight down to Cleeve [5¼ m.] rating 30. Slightly better, stream down a bit, but headwind. Tends to run down on strokeside on the beginning. Not bad for one piece on the way back past the Beetle and Wedge. Rather sluggish on the beginning.   10½ miles.

23.2.54 Buchanan came in at 4. Sorrell 4 → 2. Field 2 → Bow. Cranmer out. Rowed to Cleeve rating 30. Headwind but fairly calm. Not so good, beginnings sluggish and slow through. Crew does not seem to work for these points. Hands very slow again. Too little clearance for a rate of 30. $10\frac{1}{2}$ miles.

24.2.54 Cranmer back at Bow. Field to 7. Kitchener out. Rowed lock to lock in 34.10. Headwind. Sluggish on way down particularly before Pylons. Rate 30, down to $29\frac{1}{2}$ on the way back. Not as fast as it could be. Strokeside slow in applying work. Bowside short. 13 miles.

25.2.54 Changed crew into what is to be, barring accidents, the final order. Sorrell to stroke, Arber to 7, Porter to 6. Rand over to bowside to row 5. Buchanan remains at 4, Brasher to 3 with Field 2 and Cranmer retaining his seat at Bow.

Very strong headwind, very rough, down to Railway Bridge rating 30 and 29. Cleeve, and back in two stretches, rating down to 29 and $28\frac{1}{2}$. Finally tremendous hailstorm all the way back from Mongewell, everyone soaked and an inch of hail in bottom of boat. $10\frac{1}{2}$ miles.

26.2.54 Straight down to Cleeve at 30 except for one patch at 29, boat running quite well. Back in two pieces, encouraging, crew seems to be fitting together quite well in spite of individual faults. A good outing although could still be a lot better.

$10\frac{1}{2}$ miles.

27.2.54 Rowed lock to lock in 30.58. Oxford joined in 1 length down at the boathouse and rapidly took one length's lead. R.A.F. slowly drew up till crews were level at the beginning of Beetle and Wedge straight, then drew away to lead by two lengths at the Leather Bottle and at finish. A good row in nice, though not fast, conditions. 13 miles.
Total mileage for week: 68.

An VIII will reach its maximum cruising speed from a drifting start in about seven strokes, therefore a trained crew will go off quickly and hard for seven strokes before settling into its economical gait, that is, the maximum pace which it can hold to the end of the course. The economical gait varies from crew to crew and may be anything from 28 to 38 but it should be found out in practice well before the race. Suppose, in calm conditions, a crew's E.G. is 33 strokes per minute, this means that rowing over the course at 33 all the way they will finish up completely rowed out. At 33½ they would fold up before the end and at 32½ they would finish up with just a little energy left. Some crews prefer to go flat out for 20 strokes before settling down and others to go flat out to Barnes Bridge (about three minutes' rowing), but this is an inefficient way to row the course and betokens the crew that has not worked out its E.G., or has not the courage of its convictions. Seven strokes should be all that is needed, and a high rating after that will be more than counterbalanced at the other end of the course. If a crew has clicked into its E.G. it follows that it should not try and vary its pace or indulge in a series of spurts over the course, nor that it should be capable of a sprint at the finish; still, the race always seems to pull a little more out of the crew than they could manage in practice and I believe that a properly trained crew can knock the odd second or two off its time by taking the rate up and going 'hell for leather' down the boats at Putney. However, this is something that should not be started too early. Better to keep going at the E.G. until the 'black buoy' and then sprint the last two minutes than to start the home sprint at the mile post and to degenerate into a washy mess along the Putney embankment.

Working on the principle that frictional resistance increases as the square of the velocity and that a crew gets progressively slower at the same rate as its muscles tire the logical way to row would appear to be to maintain a uniform velocity over the course by increasing the rate steadily throughout. This requires a lot of confidence and I have only rowed in one race where it has been done. In 1953, at the Reading Head of the River, the R.A.F. VIII rowed the first half mile at 30 and the last half mile at over 40, taking the rate up about two pips every three minutes; it was an interesting experiment but it requires a tremendous amount of confidence to hold the rate down in the first mile. We actually finished two seconds behind the winners and, being rather a poor crew, justified the experiment, but we never had the courage to do it again and I would recommend the 'economical gait' method to any crew setting out to win the Head of the River race.

THE OXFORD AND CAMBRIDGE BOAT RACE

I see no reason why training for this event should be in any way different to that for the Head of the River; it is true that it is a tactical race in that the task is to beat the other crew rather than to row over the course as fast as possible, but it is still advisable to train with the latter object in mind.

Opinions vary widely as to the importance of the Boat Race and there can be no denying that, while some of the finest British crews have started as 'Blue Boats', there have been others which for all their facilities for training would not have got into the first ten in the Head of the River. To my mind this reveals the fundamental flaw in the British coaching method as typified by Boat Race training, but more about that in Chapter 5.

Perhaps speaking a little out of turn it seems to me there are two main criticisms to make about the present-day training programme. In the first place insufficient attention is paid to the development of killer instinct; probably because of the considerable Press coverage and the ballyhoo that surrounds practice, the crews are cosseted and sheltered from racing against top-line opposition. It would be of much more value for the University to learn to fight its way past a pacing crew which has slipped it, than for the pacing crew to be promptly eased as is invariably the case. Tradition dictates that full-course trials should involve several pacemakers, presumably because it is considered that no one of them should be able to remain alongside for more than a few minutes. This is rarely the case and in 1957 and 1958, for example, Oxford could well have rowed the whole course with the Isis crew, which were only slightly slower.

The result of this shielding from competition, particularly fast competition, is that many crews fail to develop the ruthless will to win that is essential to top-class racing—I was amazed on meeting one crew a few days before the race to find that they were mainly interested in what they were going to do afterwards. Needless to say, they lost.

The second weakness of current Boat Race training is that the crews are not worked hard enough. For instance, in the final three weeks it has become the custom for them to do only two full-course trials, the first of which is little more than a paddle. This is in direct contrast to the crews of fifty years ago who might do eight or ten flat-out full courses in the last month. The deterioration in technique which sets in during the race each year is an indication of the lack of racing stamina.

Short-distance races

It is possible to combine training for both short- and long-distance races and American university crews are often called upon to row in both on successive weekends with considerable success. But as the best five-mile runner is not usually best over one mile, so a crew training for short races can afford to do more shorter repetition rows and less long courses than the crew in training for long distance.

Again, it is racing stamina that is the race winner: the ability to row, without loss of power or deterioration of skill, at a racing pace for a distance at least as great as the longest course contemplated. One crew may be very fast off the mark, another may have a grandstand finishing spurt, but most races are won by the crew which has the fastest economical gait; that is, the crew that can row fastest over the course between the starting sprint and the finishing burst. Because any disparity between two crews will show up quickly in a long-distance row the pacing value is often limited and reliance has to be placed on the stop-watch to add incentive to a piece of rowing. For short stretches, though, it is advisable to work two crews together wherever possible and to reproduce the atmosphere of a race in training. There are many examples of this method proving successful, perhaps the most recent being the case of the Canadian coxless IV which won in the 1956 Olympic Games. This crew was composed of the spare men for the VIII, their rowing experience was very small and their technical skill of a low order. During practice they were always rowed with the VIII and every outing they had to row as hard as they could in order to hold them off for as long as possible. This sort of training is the best possible conditioning for racing.

During the months before the R.A.F. won the Thames Cup and Wyfolds in 1953 we used to get out in two IVs every day at 8 a.m. and every single morning we would finish with a five-minute race as hard as we could go. This to some extent made up for the VIII (which went out in the evening) having no other crews with which to practise. But I encountered the outstanding illustration of this principle in the 1954 R.A.F. IV. Formed in April, their average age was twenty, and two of the members had not rowed since the preceding summer; we had an indifferent Thames Cup VIII boating as well and every evening we did a five-mile row together, the IV taking two lengths' start. With the VIII rowing at about 30 we found the IV had to row a long powerful 29 to keep up and this had to be done at full pressure all the time. The VIII was not faster than the IV, but it was very consistent over the five miles; one bad stroke or one small mistake in steering would lose the IV a length which could never be recovered. This was the best preparation for racing that we could possibly have had and the ultimate speed of the crew, which lost to the Russians by one and a quarter lengths in the final of the Stewards' Cup—giving away five stone in a gale of a headwind before winning the silver medal at the European Championships—was an indication of the success of the method. (*See* Plate XIV, opposite page 136.)

In many ways this was one of the best crews in which I have rowed and although I have been in bigger, stronger, more experienced crews, and those that have been together for longer, none have been so well trained. Again, because it reached the international standard within a few months with material and facilities no better than that of many crews in the country, I am going to repeat some of the training log, word for word, as I recorded it in 1954.

TRAINING LOG OF THE R.A.F. IV, APRIL–MAY 1954

Crew:[1]	Bow	Sorrell
	2	Beresford
	3	Rand, W.
	Str.	Porter

26.4.54 Sunny and windy, rowed without a vest for the first time. Paddled down to Pylons in front of Trinity College Oxford VIII, then rowed the $3\frac{1}{4}$ miles to Cleeve starting IV, Trinity VIII and R.A.F. VIII all bow to stern. Terrific struggle with R.A.F. VIII who only cleared us down the last stretch, Trinity some way behind. Back, Beetle and Wedge, Pylons, then rowed in [2 m.] only half a length down on VIII starting level. $10\frac{1}{2}$ miles.

27.4.54 Strong wind, sunny. Rowed down to Pylons and picked up VIII there, paddled together to the Beetle and Wedge, R.A.F. VIII started 1 length down and finished 1 length up. We steered badly round the outside of the big bend. Then raced the VIII to Cleeve and beat them by half a length. Came back independently to Pylons stopping at the Beetle and Wedge, then raced home with VIII in 12.8 to beat them by half a length. Last piece not bad at 28–29. We tend to rush at 30–31. Many points to clear up.
          $10\frac{1}{2}$ miles.

[1]Stroke and 2 changed places before Henley.

28.4.54 Cloudy, strong wind. Hung about and picked up VIII who were rowing a lock to lock. Started 2 lengths up, but drew away to finish 4 lengths ahead taking it steady, rate about 27. Back Beetle and Wedge, Pylons, rowed in starting level with VIII, finish 4 lengths up, VIII really chronic, IV still a long way to go. Finishes washy, crew forgets to steady the sliding, steering off occasionally.   10½ miles.

29.4.54 Not quite so good. Less wind but close. Rowed Pylons at 29, Cleeve doing low rate 22–23. Came back Beetle and Wedge, Pylons, home. Somehow not quite together, boat shudders at finish, sliding not dead controlled, general slamming in from a height and 2 still washing out. Fair amount of power and better towards the end.   10½ miles.

30.4.54 Wind has swung round. Water rough in patches. Straight down to Cleeve rate 24–28, rough water shows up our faults very badly. Boat thrown about, not enough controlled relaxation, too stiff. Shown up again in following wind on the way back. Not loose enough, quick enough or skilful enough. Pylons, home.

10½ miles.

1.5.54 Very strong wind, rough water. Down to Pylons, then on ½ mile to R.E.'s Bailey Bridge being erected at Cholsey, then through to Cleeve, rating about 28. Not very clever in rough water, awful slog into headwind. Not too bad coming back in following wind though still not quite relaxed and not quick enough in. Cholsey, Pylons and home. Very tired.   10½ miles.

2.5.54 No outing. Marked out practice Henley course with a length of string.
Total mileage for week: 63.

3.5.54 Raining. Cold but less wind. Water mainly calm. Straight down to Cleeve with the VIII, they were about 3 lengths faster, most of which we lost on steering. Very hard work at 29½–30 to keep up with them. Poorish on the way back at 24. Easied at Island, Pylons, not nearly enough concentration, not controlled, chopping in. Better on the row in [2 m.] in 12.30. Not fast conditions. We go better when the rate is above 28.   10½ miles.

4.5.54 Raining, cold, moderate wind. Raced VIII to Cleeve, starting 2 lengths up and finishing 3 lengths down, they having given us a length round the island. Probably half this was lost on steering. Still working for control and steady sliding. Not bad in patches when we think about it, but slack when we stop concentrating. Back Railway Bridge, home, must concentrate far more. VIII much faster.   10½ miles.

5.5.54 Very strong wind, extremely rough. Paddled down to Mongewell in pairs, decided it was too rough and turned and paddled up to Benson Lock. We do not go at all well in rough water. Gave up after 4 miles as soaked to the skin and boat half full of water.   4 miles.

6.5.54 Strong wind but fairly calm, short outing as have to get back to Camp early. Straight down to Beetle and Wedge and back rating about 30. Not too good, steering bad and too little control on the way forward, boat very dead at times probably due to stiffness forward and not coming down to the water on the beginning we tend to 'sky' and so waste effort.   8 miles.

7.5.54 Good conditions at last, calm with slight breeze. Paddled straight down to Cleeve in one piece, rate 30, 29½, 30 finishing at 34, much better, fair stride and less stiffening. Came back, Railway Bridge, Pillbox and home, rating 29, quite enjoyable after the last few outings. 2 more solid on his lowered rigger. Encouraging.
                                      10½ miles.

8.5.54 Sunny, warm, light wind. Morning outing. Picked up VIII who were rowing a lock to lock and rowed straight through to Cleeve, started 2 lengths up and were leading by about 8 lengths when they decided to easy at the Beetle and Wedge. Rate 29. Back in three pieces, boat going quite fast but hard into headwind, and not quite loose enough in following wind.   10½ miles. Total mileage for week: 54.

Tactical racing: two abreast

There used to be, and (for all I know) still is, a saying that you should go all out to beat the other crew in the first minute or, failing that, in the second minute, and so on. This may be successful for scratch and inexperienced crews, and for those whose training has been over a much longer course than that in the race, but it is hardly a sensible way to row in a first-class event.

Even in two-abreast races it is the crew with the faster economical gait that usually wins and it is only when both are fairly evenly matched that tactics can decide the result: there is then an almost infinite number of variations that one can adopt. One favourite is to go off very fast to snatch a lead and then to sit and watch your opponent, answering any spurt as it dies away. Some crews prefer to sit slightly down and row past at a predetermined point, while others just settle down to row the course as fast as possible.

Each method has much to be said for it and it is impossible to do more than generalize. The first is probably best against inexperienced oarsmen, who may get rattled to find themselves left behind at the start. The second can be very successful against an experienced but not very fit crew and the third is best against very well-drilled crews and those adopting the first method.

Probably the only way to discuss tactics is to take actual races. The method favoured by most American crews, particularly between five and twelve years ago, was to settle into an economical gait from the start and row past their opponents during the second half of the course. This had the big psychological advantage that other crews, being aware of their strong finish, would tend to scramble over the first half to build up a big lead. One such race was the semi-final of the Thames Cup in 1953 between Princeton University and the R.A.F.; we set out with the intention of taking a lead during the first half of the course and putting the rate up two strokes per minute at Fawley. The result was that we had one length's lead at Fawley, but to achieve that we had had to row at 35 instead of our economical gait of 33½; we then put up the rate to 37 and squeezed another quarter of a length. At Remenham, Princeton started their famous spurt and came at us, and having rowed ourselves out we had no answer; somehow, we got it up to 38 at the Mile Post with Princeton at 40 and, thanks to our fitness and determination, we scraped home a third of a length ahead. In the final we rowed down our opponents, Imperial College, at the Mile Post striking our economical gait of 33½ and won by half a length. Afterwards, it was generally agreed that our tactics against Princeton had paid off and they themselves admitted that our putting a quarter of a length of daylight between us between Fawley and Remenham had come as a shock; however, the intermediate times of the two races, rowed in identical conditions, tell their own story:

	Barrier	Fawley	Finish
Semi-final v. Princeton ..	1.59	3.23	7.05
Final v. Imperial College ..	2.02*	3.25*	6.59

* I.C. leading.

The fact is that our own finishing spurt should have been more than a match for Princeton's had we had the courage to row the semi-final as we rowed the final.

The dangers of sitting on a lead are numerous, but two outstanding examples come to mind. One was in the first round of the Stewards' Cup in 1951 when L.M.B.C. led Thames R.C. all the way down the course, striking 26 to Thames' 31. Up the enclosures Thames spurted to 38 and rowed past the L.M.B.C. IV who had settled into such a long efficient stroke that they were unable to raise their rate above 29, even when losing by two feet. The second concerns the Olympic trial race for coxless pairs in 1952. Bywater and Christie led Davidge and Callender by two to three lengths at Remenham, when Davidge put in a tremendous spurt and rowed 40 all the way to the finish. Bywater and Christie had settled into too high a gear and, being unable to snap out of it, were rowed down before they hit the booms just short of the finish. In such a case it is advisable to shorten for three strokes to jump the rate up, but this they could not do.

Most crews that are credited with a strong finish have in reality not so much a fast spurt as a uniform paced economical gait. This was the case with the R.A.F. Stewards' IV in 1954 against Kobenhavns Roklub. In each of the two previous heats the Danish crew had sprinted past their opponents at Remenham, having been led up till then, but we decided to try and beat them at their own game. They led us three-quarters of a length off the start but had to keep going at 38 to hold their lead, while we were cruising at our economical rate of 35; the pace was too hot and we had the satisfaction of seeing them crack up at Remenham, the very point where they had beaten their previous opponents.

As I said before, tactics will not help a crew to win unless they are in the running anyway, but there have been occasions where tactics have served to beat an only slightly better crew. One such case in which I was involved was in 1952 in the Wyfolds when I was rowing in an unfit crew. Our opponents should have beaten us on form but they were not such seasoned racers. We slipped them on the start, taking three-quarters of a length, and, between the first signal and Remenham (with a better stride), they slowly rowed past us to lead by half a length. As prearranged we slammed everything into a 20-stroke spurt at the Mile Post and went past to lead by half a length again, by which time we had shot our bolt. However, our opponents were so upset at losing in twenty strokes what it had taken them over half the course to gain that they had a slight shipwreck and, after they had recovered, did not quite manage to catch us again before the finish. I might add that we were soundly beaten in the semi-final by a much faster crew against whom no tactics would have helped.

Planning tactics before the race is great fun but there is no denying that the best one of all is to develop a fast cruising pace during training.

Economical gait: three or more crews abreast

There are few races for three crews abreast in this country and, as far as I know, none for four or more; this means that British crews selected to compete in international regattas are often at a disadvantage.

The only sure-fire method to row a multiple race is to cover the course in the shortest possible time, and the best way to train for this is to row the set distance against the stop-watch, noting the times at certain intervals: preferably a quarter, half and three-quarter way. This does not mean that one should plan to row each quarter in exactly the same time, but that, allowing for starting sprints, finishing bursts and physical deterioration, the optimum relative speeds for each part of the course should be ascertained during training, and practised until they become second nature. The dangers of treating international championship events as tactical races are all too obvious. To highlight this point I might mention a *repêchage* heat of the coxless IVs in the European Championships, 1954. The R.A.F. were drawn in lane one, with Germany, who we thought to be our most dangerous rivals, in lane two. The Russian crew, which was rather slow, was next, with the Rumanian IV on the far side. We rowed neck and neck with the Germans to about the 1,250 metres, by which time the Russians were several lengths astern, and then the Germans blew up and we took a three-quarters of a length in 10 strokes. Instinctively we kept going hard and it was as well we did for at the 1,500 metres a glance showed that the Rumanians, who were almost invisible under the bank on the far side, were actually leading us by a few feet and we had to pull out a storming finish to beat them. Had we known that this same Rumanian crew were to win the gold medal the following year no doubt we would have watched them from the start.

The classic example must, however, be the heat in the single sculls in the 1948 Olympics between Risso of Uruguay, Kelly of U.S.A. and Rowe of Great Britain. Kelly and Rowe had a tremendous private battle with Risso trailing more than two lengths astern at halfway, but they were exceeding their economical gait and by 1,500 metres Risso, who had been sculling at his best pace, passed Rowe, who had virtually sculled himself out, and went on to catch Kelly on the post, winning by a few feet.

To sit and row at one's economical gait when every other crew has sprinted away in front requires the confidence which can only come from repeated drilling. I remember one American (I think it was D. D. Cadle, who rowed for Balliol College, Oxford, in 1953) telling me of a coxed IV which he rowed in for the 1948 Olympic trials. They had only a few weeks to prepare and every night they would row course after course, the cox sitting with a stopwatch on his knee. Their coach had worked out exactly how long each 250 metres should take them for the conditions and at each signal their cox would tell them if they were up or down or on time. When they came to race they often found themselves four or five lengths down at halfway, yet they always rowed past to win in the end. This crew only lost to Washington University, who went on to win the Olympics, by a small margin in the final of the American Olympic trials.

For a crew to enter for a three or more abreast race without knowing what rating it must strike at each part of the course, and what its relative times to each signal must be, is simply asking to be beaten.

The mental approach

To prepare for a race it is not sufficient simply to train the body to move the boat as fast as possible over the course, it is necessary to tune the mind to race as well. I will go further and say that if an oarsman is not imbued with an over-riding urge to win he will not physically give of his best during the race.

The oarsman's appetite for winning must be insatiable, he should be out for blood and no shadow of compassion or sympathy for the other crew allowed to cross his mind; winning the race by any fair means within his power must at all times be uppermost.

How is it possible to develop killer instinct in a crew? Preferably by repeated competition between two or more crews. Race them together as much as possible, praising the winners, reproving the losers. If they are first and second crews of the same club change the oarsmen around, relegating anyone who does not seem to be trying his hardest; encourage the crews to hate each other when they are out on the water; let it be freely known that getting there first is the only criterion of good rowing. In this way racing spirit develops along with improved performance. If there is no other crew of comparable standard against which to practise, the problem is a little more difficult and can best be solved by encouraging personal competition either in smaller boats or in out-of-the-boat activities. In the R.A.F., where we usually had the VIII on its own, we did this by splitting into two coxless IVs and racing each other. We also had a sculling league, everyone racing in turn in a pair of matched rum-tums down to the lock and back: a distance of 10 miles. We raced each other when we ran and we matched ourselves in practically every form of physical training we did. If you beat somebody at something you jeered at him. This encouraged him to try and beat you next time.

There can be disadvantages in this method, as we discovered when we had to separate two men who were attempting to mutilate each other just before a race at Henley, but I believe that the crew raced with more fighting spirit as a result than if they had been amiable and contented.

There is one oarsman renowned for his racing spirit who,

some years ago when he was competing for his juniors, found himself stroking a clinker four in the final having already rowed several races that day. On the first stroke his blade lodged under a mass of weed which was so heavy that he could not move it and, being utterly weary, he stopped. No. 3 not having witnessed this, but seeing their opponents vanishing in the distance, let out a pained 'Come *on*!' and the stroke, incensed at being thus reproached, lost his temper and, tearing his blade from the water, weed and all, set off at a rate of 44 down the course. They rapidly overhauled and passed the other crew but still kept going at 44 until they reached the finish, several lengths ahead, where the stroke collapsed. They had to carry him from the boat and put him to bed, moreover he was unable to row again for a fortnight thanks probably to a fighting spirit aroused, not against his opponents, but against the member of his crew who had doubted his determination.

If any oarsman has his killer instinct developed to this extent he is invaluable in any crew.

Racing is a cold, ruthless business and it is said that one famous sculler was not above shouting 'Look-ahead!' to his opponent when he felt he might be beaten. But that does not mean that pleasantries must not be exchanged before the race. A useful dodge against an inexperienced opponent is to complain that the crew is not going well or does not feel like racing. Sometimes a pathetically slow practice start is sufficient to lull them into a complacent frame of mind before you go off like a bullet. I have known an oarsman in an opposing crew turn round and shout, 'We're *not*!' when our cox had been telling us that they were getting scrappy; these things are all worth the odd second.

There are those who like to indulge in a 'hate' session before an important race, each man expounding on some feature of the other crew (one not necessarily based on reality). But I believe that a crew that has been taught to race as if they were fighting for their lives will have no need for such artificial devices. Ideally I think they should set out with the intention of quietly grinding their opposition into the dust and this attitude should not be relaxed until the winning post has been reached.

5

Coaching

What makes a good coach?

MY COACHING experience has been small and if it has taught me anything it is that I shall never learn all there is to know about it. On the other hand I have been coached by a great number of people and I think I can honestly say that this has taught me a good deal about what makes a bad coach.

Probably no man who cycles along the towpath or rides in the launch knows exactly what effect he has on his crew and if many coaches, who fondly imagine that their crews are lapping up every word, knew what they were really thinking they would give up at once. This toleration of mediocre coaches is one of the odd features of British rowing. I have asked a number of oarsmen why they put up with various coaches who do not appear to know the first thing about rowing, and their answers have been fascinating, but the commonest explanation is that they think a bad coach is better than none at all. They will agree that the man talks pure drivel; they will agree that he has been saying the same things for twenty years; they will even agree that he has never produced a fast crew in his life, and yet they believe that they have a better outing with 'someone on the bank'. I can only conclude that such crews are so mentally idle, or incapable of constructive thought on their own behalf, that they would rather have someone else doing the (possibly wrong) thinking for them, at whatever cost, than work things out for themselves.

What, then, makes a good coach? Above all, I think—honesty. He must be honest with his crew or he will lose their confidence and once he has done this he is valueless. I am reminded of a certain coach who was in many ways brilliant. He had a distinguished rowing career; he was versatile, intelligent and witty. His enthusiasm was infectious and he gave his crews a wonderful sense of purpose. He could take on a crew that was without hope and bring it up to international standard, but he was not 100 per cent honest with it. If they were going through a bad spell in training he would tell them so and how he thought they could correct it, but he would never do it the day before the big race. Then he was always confident: they were going well; they would eat the race; the boat had never moved faster. If his crew won, everything was all right—oarsmen are ever ready to be persuaded they are rowing well. But if they lost . . . ! He had but to put his foot wrong once and he would be finished with that crew for good. If he told them that they were always going faster and faster, and it was proved beyond all doubt that they had, in fact, been going slower and slower, none of the oarsmen in that crew would ever trust him again.

Perhaps some will disagree with me, but I think that a coach must be scrupulously honest both with himself and his crew. This does not mean that he necessarily has to be right. If he says to his crew, 'I think you are going faster than you were last week and if you row sensibly you should win'—this being his honest opinion—his crew can lose and still have faith in him, for, after all, the result does depend to some extent on the speed of the other crew. But even the dumbest oarsman is quick to detect dishonesty in a coach and it is not worth the risk.

Second to honesty I should rate enthusiasm. A coach must show enthusiasm towards his crew, or he cannot expect them to have any. If he is enthusiastic about their chances he can row them till they drop, he can curse them and 'kick them to death' from the bank; if he is really keen about them they will take courage from him, for they will say to themselves, 'If he believes so strongly in us and is prepared to put in so much of his time to helping us we must have some chance.'

A good coach must become like one of the crew; he should be prepared to give up as much time to it as they do and he must throw himself heart and soul behind them; he must resolve to do better when they row badly and he can rejoice when they row well; together they will suffer agonies waiting for the start of the race and, with them, the coach sweats out a tight finish. A good deal of enthusiasm will more than make up for lack of technical knowledge in any coach.

Lastly, there is the technical knowledge itself. This can come with years of experience. I was told that at one American university they tested every oarsman on a machine to see who could pull the hardest and found the eight hardest shovers had already been selected by the experienced professional coach and were, in fact, the 'varsity crew!

Probably anyone who likes to think about rowing, and has taken the trouble to watch and appraise first-class crews, will make a competent coach if he is prepared to learn as he goes along. In fact, many people start coaching almost as soon as they start rowing. For example, at schools and colleges members of the first boat are called upon to coach house crews and lower boats. This is an excellent way to start, for any oarsman can learn a lot by coaching others while it will do a coach a lot of good to sit in a boat and learn how instruction comes over at the other end.

Many oarsmen get through a successful rowing career without appearing to realize the basic requirements of a fast crew, and it is an interesting fact that two of the men with the most successful records are appallingly bad coaches and judges of crews. On the other hand, many of the best coaches will admit that they were no great shakes as oarsmen and Hiram

Conibear, the highly successful Washington coach credited with the origination of the present American style, is said to have been a baseball coach who never touched an oar.

Anyone who is really keen on rowing, and will take the trouble to think a little about it and keep an open mind, can become a competent coach.

Crew selection

Some clubs are 'lucky' in that they only have four or eight men who are prepared to row, and the problem of selection does not arise. Oxford and Cambridge, on the other hand, may have a hundred oarsmen from which to select their crew and it must be very rare for them to pick the fastest combination. So many factors may influence the selection in such a case that the task requires detailed knowledge of the men available. For example, A may be a hard shover with poor technique: can he be taught to row? B exhibits immaculate form but never shoves very hard: can he be persuaded to shove? Oarsmen may be rejected because they are so set in their ways that they can never improve; some may be unwilling to try; some develop antisocial tendencies as the race approaches; others are apt to break down under test.

I think it is best to look out for the enthusiast and the tryer, as it is this sort of oarsman who responds best to training. Anyone who is lukewarm at the start of training (excluding the novice oarsman) is unlikely to stay the course. Physical strength is, of course, important but a thirteen-stone, 6 ft. 4 in. colossus is best rejected if he is not prepared to put everything into his rowing.

I understand that the late Professor Cotton, of the Physiology Department at Sydney University, devised a rowing machine on which oarsmen are selected for the Sydney R.C. crew. Every man rows on this for fifteen minutes, building up a total number of points via a complicated gearing system. The machine is adjusted before he starts to compensate for his weight, and a further factor is included at the end to allow for the fact that a heavy oarsman imparts more momentum to the boat than a lighter one. The crew is normally made up of the eight oarsmen to produce the highest total unless there are other exceptional considerations.

There is a lot to be said for this method inasmuch as it rules out a lot of the prejudices with which anyone faced with crew selection has to contend. But a better system is that practised in the American universities where the crews are raced side by side every day, men being changed one by one until the fastest combination results.

In my opinion the latter method must produce the faster crew. With the former, the coach may find himself presented with four large men who are most effective rowing a long, efficient stroke at a rate of, say, 32, and four small men who have achieved selection by rowing a short economical stroke at a rate of, say, 38. Though individually the eight best oarsmen, they would not be likely to prove the fastest combination in the end.

My own preference is for a strong determined man who will row hard even if he does not row well, for the chances are that he can be taught to row, at least effectively, far quicker than a polished oarsman can acquire strength and what, for want of a better word, I will call 'guts'. Having neither a rowing machine nor sufficient oarsmen for more than one complete crew in the R.A.F., we adopted the system of putting the experienced men in the bows of the VIII in the early stages of training, and trying out all the newcomers in the stern. We would then row at a racing rhythm for several miles and watch to see how effective they became when they began to get really tired. We were surprised to discover by this method that some men on whom we had been counting became very short, washy or weak, while others whom we had tended to write off kept poling the boat along with plenty of determination.

There is one danger to be guarded against in selecting a crew, and that is what is known as a 'boat-stopper'. These men may be difficult to detect; they may seem keen and they may be big and strong and appear to row well, but any boat in which they row unaccountably goes slower as the race approaches and their rating increases. I think the fundamental flaw with such oarsmen is that they are physically slow-moving and unable to co-ordinate their actions at a racing rate. A man of this type may be impressive paddling at 22 strokes to the minute; if the crew he is rowing in can steady down to 28 in a race he can still look convincing rowing up the enclosures, but when he is called upon to row really hard at, maybe, 34, his movements are so slow that he is a fraction late on the beginning, he tends to tear out his finish and he comes thundering down the slide to stop the boat dead on the frontstop. More than likely he will be the first to complain after the race is lost, and his complaint will usually be that he did not have enough time and that if they had gathered a bit more over the stretcher they would have gone a lot faster.

Every crew will have its weakness. Ask any coach and he will say: 'It is a really fine crew except for 4. If only we had a really strong man to put in at 4 we should be all right'; the chances are that if he had a really good man at 4 he would be saying the same thing about 3 or 7. The danger with this attitude is that if one or two of the other men drop out for one reason or another the coach is left with a crew which, on his own admission, contains too many weak links to become really fast. Better to assume that all the oarsmen are potentially first-class and that good coaching will produce a top-line crew, for it is worth remembering that, in 1956, the University of British Columbia had thirteen oarsmen only in the rowing club—four of them won a gold medal in the Melbourne Olympics and eight of them a silver medal.

Bringing up a crew

I use this phrase deliberately, for developing pace throughout training is rather like bringing up a child: one must teach the crew the basic essentials, the three 'Rs' of rowing, if you like, then one must coax it and train it and periodically examine it on its ability. One must cope with its tantrums and hold its hand when it is afraid; oarsmen in training are like children in many ways.

When a coach is presented with a collection of oarsmen at the beginning of training and told to make a crew of them, he has, at the outset, to decide which of the two fundamental approaches he is to adopt, given that in the end a fast crew is going to row an efficient stroke at a racing rate (30 or above).

There is the normal English way which fits the oarsmen together and coaches them into rowing well as a crew at a fairly low rate, say about 20. The tempo is then slowly raised, the crew at the same time maintaining their length and efficiency as the rating increases until eventually they are able to row as well at 34, or whatever the racing pace of the crew is, as when they had been taught to row at 18–20.

The other method which is, or was, popular in America is to demand a racing rate (27 or above) from the crew at the outset and to develop their technique and all-round ability at that rate. Each method, properly executed, arrives at the same end product: a crew capable of rowing efficiently at a high rate; but for a number of reasons I prefer the second method, and briefly stated these are:

1. Strength and stamina are developed much more quickly.
2. Individuals who are incapable of driving themselves really hard show up much sooner.
3. The crew is ready to race much earlier.
4. It entails no 'peak' of training and therefore crews are unlikely to 'go over the top' or fail to achieve their best performance by the time of the race, as in the first method.

Amplifying this last point, what frequently happens with the normal English crew is that, having spent the requisite period developing their technique at 20 strokes to the minute, they then have to step up their rate at, say, two pips a week. All goes well for the first two weeks but then illness or some other factor holds up improvement for a week, and they arrive at the race rowing at two strokes a minutes less than was planned. Alternatively, having rowed one race at the 'peak', what is the crew to do about subsequent races? It is clearly impossible to go on raising the rate week by week throughout the rest of the season. Unless the coach is to switch to method two, which can be unsettling, he has to try and hold them where they are, which is very hard, or take them down a few pips and bring them back again.

By starting at a racing rhythm the performance of the crew can be improved indefinitely as they learn to row harder and with more efficiency. No hard and fast peak is aimed at so that the crew never go 'over the top' or get stale.

To adopt method two, which I am sure produces better results in a shorter time, it is necessary for the coach to be very hard-hearted at the beginning. An American friend, who rowed at the U.S. Naval Academy, told me that in the second week of training (not having rowed for several months) the crew would be set to row for five miles at 30 strokes per minute and if the rate dropped below this, even for an instant, they were sent back to the start to do it again. Naturally, a crew told to do this does not go very fast at first, and in point of fact would probably have gone faster striking 20, but having once decided on this course the coach must be firm and stick to his guns, regardless of derision.

I remember that when the R.A.F. started training in November 1953 the Oxford trial VIIIs had already been rowing several weeks. In a two-mile race one of these crews, striking 22, beat us by over ten lengths although our rate did not drop below 29. Six weeks later when we were both striking 29 we returned the compliment and took several lengths off them. It is all a matter of having confidence in the method.

Another advantage of always training over long distances at a racing rate is that it makes the crew's performance very consistent. They still have good rows and bad rows but the bad rows are not much slower than the good rows. Also, it is very easy to tune up for a race: suppose the crew rows ten miles an outing averaging 30 strokes per minute and two 'easies'—all one has to do ten days before the race is to cut the outings down to, say, seven miles, increase the number of easies per outing to five, and the crew will be bursting with suppressed energy, anxious to pack more and more into each stroke they row. After the race it is easy to resume the original training programme until the next big race looms ahead.

One afterthought: as a result of my experience in coaching the Oxford crew of 1958 I do not think it is possible to combine the two methods. Gavin Sorrell, the President of the O.U.B.C., who had experienced both systems of training, very courageously tried to get the best of both worlds by asking L. A. F. Stokes, Grp. Capt. H. R. A. Edwards, myself and J. H. Page to take the four successive periods. All four of us had achieved some measure of success as coaches in the previous twelve months and the oarsmen themselves were individually above average for Boat Race material, so that the failure of the crew was significant.

They were started under the English system of low ratings and short stretches and, by the time that Grp. Capt. Edwards handed the VIII over to me, they were at about the same stage as most Boat Race crews at the end of five weeks. We then switched to doing greater mileage at a racing pitch with an aggregate of thirty minutes' rowing a day, and at the end of a month they were making good progress. However, in the last four weeks a return to low ratings and short stretches did not bring the crew on at all and in the end I was certain that any one of the four coaches would have achieved a better result by himself.

I might add that the scathing comments of various newspaper correspondents, most of whom live in the world of thirty years ago, did little to encourage what was, I think, a useful, if unsuccessful, experiment.

Physiological aspects of coaching

It goes without saying that a coach should have the physical well-being of his crew at heart, and should see that they do not suffer any discomfort other than that inherent in rowing. On the other hand it is not really being kind to terminate an outing simply because the crew 'look worn out'. Training is essentially conditioning of the body to withstand fatigue and this can only be done by continuing to drill the crew when deterioration due to fatigue has set in. A fifteen-mile outing is no more exhausting to an oarsman who is used to fifteen-mile outings than a five-mile one to the oarsman who is used to five miles. But given that the amount of work to be done in the boat must not be reduced, there are a number of points which the good coach should watch. Of the first importance is a short period at the beginning and end of every outing devoted to relaxed, easy paddling. No sane track-runner would commence his training with a sprint round the course, nor would he stop short when his serious training was over and go straight in for his shower. Before he started his track work he would probably jog round several circuits in a track suit until all the stiffness and tenseness was thrown off and his muscles were ready for their task. Similarly, a few more gentle circuits at the end would serve to wind down the body from the peak to which it had been tuned. So in the boat I advocate that crews spend a short time at the beginning and end of every outing in loose, relaxed paddling when the object is not to move the boat fast, or even to row well, but either to get the crew warm and sweating slightly, and to gear up the heart and lungs for the increased effort, or to relax tense muscles at the end of the row.

The length of time to be spent in warming up depends upon the temperature and the frequency with which the crew is rowing. In the winter, if the weather is very cold and the crew is only boating at weekends, two or three miles may be desirable; at Henley, when the crew is out twice a day, only 20 or 30 strokes may be necessary. The National Provincial Bank crew, which I coached in 1957, normally did about half a mile of easy paddling before the outing proper and they averred that, however tired or stiff they felt when they first stepped into the boat, by the time they had 'doodled' half a mile they were ready to go and were loose and 'on their feet'. If they had left the stage briskly and tried to row hard at once, before their hearts and lungs were ready, the chances are that they would have been breathless and the boat would have gone badly from the outset.

This brings us on to the question of warmth in general. As a result of rowing in freezing weather, clad only in vest and shorts, I am convinced that really cold weather saps muscular strength more rapidly than anything. I do not advocate going to the lengths of one well-known sculler, who went out wearing a complete fur-lined flying suit, but I do not think any oarsman can expect optimum performance from his muscles if they are exposed to very low temperatures. Track suits are rather too thick and heavy for comfortable rowing, and in any case the folds get in the way, but a thin cotton windcheater is good and a woollen sweater has the dual advantage of being form-fitting and letting perspiration evaporate freely. For the legs, athletes recommend ballet tights, but I have found a pair of long cotton underpants worn beneath the shorts cheaper and more hardwearing. Wearing these I can honestly say I have never been really cold while rowing, however low the temperature.

Coming back to the coach's responsibility, it is indefensible for him to keep a crew sitting about for long in really bitter weather. After five minutes they will have lost all interest in what he is saying in an increasing awareness of the cold wind. It seems obvious and yet it is something which happens frequently.

One should be considerate of an oarsman's minor injuries but not so as to encourage him to become morbid or to indulge in self-pity. An oarsman I once rowed with had thirty-seven blisters on his hands at one time (we counted them) and he only exhibited them out of a sense of pride, although most oarsmen so afflicted would have taken up football.

Some oarsmen do tend to mollycoddle themselves and take a day off if they have a slight chill. The principle I have worked to (without casualty) is that a man is fit to row unless he has a temperature; this means that if he catches an ordinary cold he can go on rowing but if he goes down with influenza he should lay off for a while. It is up to the doctor when he should start again after having a temperature. I once rowed with a temperature of 101 and I remember that, after a few miles, tears of weakness were running down my cheeks—on the whole I do not think it is worth it.

A good coach must not exclude himself, from the point of view of personal effort, from what I have said earlier about the need for proper outings and planned training. It is not playing the game to give a crew six-mile outings while the coach is cycling along the towpath, and twenty-mile ones when he has a launch! He must guard against regulating the outing to suit himself because the weather is inclement or he is tired of cycling. Better to give them the necessary work and catch them up when he can then have the crew come back on the tide doing three strokes at a time so that he can keep up; no coaching in the world is that valuable.

Psychological aspects of coaching

A good coach must understand the oarsmen in his crew and he will have to learn how to get the best out of them. Some oarsmen are incorrigibly idle and will need to be urged again and again to row harder; others try so hard that their movements become violent and jerky or they lose length by stiffening up, and these will have to be coaxed rather than bullied.

Somehow a coach must persuade his crew that he knows all the answers, so that they have confidence in his judgement and are prepared to do all that he asks, although it may result in the boat temporarily going slower. A case in point is when the crew is made to cover considerable distances each day at a racing rate; sheer weariness will often result in a loss of pace, particularly towards the end of the outing, and it is then that the coach has to become a 'confidence man' and sell his views to the crew.

This necessity for keeping a crew interested in their rowing and confident in their training programme is most important, for once they lose confident they will become stale. Staleness in a crew is originally a mental sickness brought about by loss of heart, so it never afflicts the crew who believe strongly in their particular system of training as producing the best results.

Once the oarsman has lost the urge to row he becomes listless and his rowing lacks fire; very often he loses weight and looks overdrawn into the bargain. If this happens, and it is detected early, a change of programme or a reshuffle of the crew sometimes has the desired effect, but if staleness becomes well advanced a few days' sculling or small-boating, or even a time away from the river altogether, should do the trick. If the coach decides to get away from the river completely for a spell it is essential that some other outdoor activity is substituted for rowing. Nothing is worse than to let the oarsmen wander about with nothing to do, moping about the progress of the crew.

Getting a crew satisfactorily through the prolonged hard work stage requires careful planning. A good method is to move the crew around frequently, preferably making all the men row on both sides; this introduces an element of change and allows plenty of hard work without their becoming bored. With the National Provincial Bank VIII I had stroke and 7 moved to 2 and bow every fortnight, the rest of the crew moving forward a place, but this is only really practicable with a fairly even weight distribution.

Even if they have confidence in their training, when they are covering about ten miles a day and including plenty of courses, they will find that, after a few weeks, they suddenly run into an utterly weary patch. I used to call this the 'seventh-week agony' because it usually came after we had been doing intensive rowing every day for about seven weeks. Once through this period it should be much better, and, with the imminence of regattas and tuning-up outings, it becomes easy. If any break in training prevents the onset of 'seventh-week agony' the crew will probably never achieve their fastest pace.

If a crew has been properly trained the final period before the racing should see the coach become almost another man. From being a ruthless, demanding slave-driver he should become bland, cheerful and confident. Whereas before he had, all too often, to remind the crew of the nearness and importance of the race, now they are very well aware of it themselves and will need comforting.

The attitude a coach should adopt just before the race is largely a matter for him to decide, depending on the nature of his crew. Generally he should be optimistic and calm, pointing out what he wants them to remember in the race and trying to give an idea of what he thinks will be the weakness of the opposition. Dramatic speeches and flag-waving are not much use before the race; a few quiet words of advice will be much more effective.

Ciné-films

It has always escaped my understanding why we in this country make so little use of ciné-films as an aid to coaching. Very few crews include them in their coaching programme and none, as far as I know, carry the matter to its logical conclusion and have a short film taken at regular intervals throughout the season. Yet two minutes with a ciné-camera can often achieve what two years of assiduous coaching cannot: firstly convincing the oarsman that he is committing some fault and secondly, as often as not, making it obvious why he is doing it. Slow motion is very good for this, for although the quickness of the hand deceives the eye it does not deceive the camera running on slow motion. Often an oarsman has developed some common fault which no amount of coaching can eradicate; in slow motion it may be seen that this is the direct result of doing something else earlier in the stroke. Once this has been appreciated by the oarsman and the coach they can set about curing the basic fault together.

Oarsmen are always prepared to believe that they have remedied some flaw when they have not in fact done so. Sometimes coaches are lazy and having spent some weeks drilling a point home, without success, they give up and go on to something else. A regular short film of the crew will remind the oarsmen of the faults they still possess. I have been as guilty as anyone could on this score. In 1953 I was stroking an VIII in which everyone said I was sticking at the finish; I was sure I was not until I saw a film of the crew—then I not only knew that my hands were sticking at the finish, but I realized why they were. Again, in 1956, I had been told at the beginning of the season that I was swinging on the frontstop, and having spent many weeks working at this point I was sure I had completely cured it—until I saw a ciné-film of the crew!

A ciné-film is a very good substitute for a coach if the oarsmen concerned are prepared to offer constructive criticism on their own rowing; moreover, however difficult it may be to get a first-class coach down to spend a whole afternoon with the crew, few men are so busy that they cannot spend half an hour in the comfortable seclusion of the clubhouse going through the film and pointing out the individual and collective weaknesses.

When the R.A.F. were experimenting on American lines we obtained a film of an extremely good Harvard crew. We saw this film through again and again, analysing the actions and trying to imagine ourselves rowing in an VIII of that sort. Later we had a film taken of ourselves and we showed them alternately several times each night until we were certain where our weaknesses lay. Later on in the season a second film showed to what extent we had improved in our technique.

To be of any use a ciné-film must be taken from a launch moving parallel to the racing boat, for the changing angles and short sequences that one gets from the bank are of little value. To get the most out of the film the camera should remain fixed on one part of the crew for at least five strokes, this being the minimum time it takes to assimilate a point. I like the camera to move in for a while and do a sequence on each pair in turn, then to move away and concentrate on bow four and stern four, and finally to go even further away and get the whole crew in for a short stretch. Ideally the camera should be right opposite the object being photographed, as shots taken obliquely and from behind are far less revealing.

I have gone into some detail on the type of film that should be taken because one usually has to compete with the artistic instincts of the photographer; he will probably want to make a beautiful film with the right patches of light and shade; to him, a film concentrating on two oarsmen rowing the same sort of stroke five times will be terribly dull and he will want to break it up with snatches of the scenery, the swans and the coxwain. Ciné-film is expensive and one must stifle these aberrations at the start.

A film need not be long to be instructive; four minutes'

running time is about the bare minimum but eight minutes for an VIII is quite satisfactory. Using 8-mm. film the cost of this, at the time of writing, is rather less than £3 inclusive, which probably compares favourably with the cost of hiring the launch; but whereas an outing with a coach is soon forgotten the lessons that can be learnt from a ciné-film last for ever.

Sculling

It may be thought odd that I should include some remarks on sculling in a chapter devoted to coaching. Let me say at once that my knowledge of sculling is very slight, but I do know enough about it to realize that it can be a valuable help in coaching a crew. This, then, is what I am going to deal with: sculling, not as it affects the man learning to scull, but the man learning to row.

Few coaches encourage their oarsmen to scull and very few would think of including sculling in their training programme for the crew. Yet after a long spell of rowing nothing redirects an oarsman's attention to the fundamental principles of boat-moving more than going out in a sculling boat. Faults like rowing the blade at the water, not striking on to the balance at the finish and hurrying forward over the stretcher are easily developed in the VIII and often pass without notice, whereas an outing in a shell sculling boat will make them rapidly apparent.

Many interesting things occur to an oarsman trying out single sculling for the first time. Clumsiness instantly causes the boat to roll; bearing down over the stretcher dips the stern and stops the boat dead—he can see it happen. In fact, before long he will see that the only way to make a sculling boat move fast is not to disturb the run of the boat in any way when the sculls are out of the water, and to row a clean, solid, powerful stroke when the blades are in the water: a technique which is well designed to move any boat. He will also find that, once he has got the feel of a sculling boat, it is just as hard work as it is rowing in a crew—very often it is harder, and if he has watched the apparently effortless ease of a really good sculler this may come as a shock to him. The advantage of sculling to the oarsman is that every feature of his rowing is amplified. He may swing out of the boat when he is rowing and the lurch is absorbed by the rest of the crew, he may smack at the water or row through half covered and still the VIII moves quite fast. But let him do these things in a 'toothpick' and he will not get away with it, moreover there is no one else to blame if the boat pitches or stops. On the other hand a really good stroke will register itself in a way that it will never do in a larger boat.

Perhaps before I wax too enthusiastic I had better come down to earth. There is at present a great deal of ballyhoo about sculling to which I do not subscribe. It is said that a crew of good scullers will beat a crew of good oarsmen any day and this is arrant nonsense. A crew of scullers derives its pace from three things: firstly they have a sense of watermanship and balance which makes for a comfortable crew, secondly they must be prepared to drive themselves to row hard or they would never become good scullers and thirdly they are usually a lot fitter than the average oarsman, particularly in winter. Of these three reasons the last is far and away the main cause of their success. A good sculler takes a much greater personal interest in his own strength and fitness than the average oarsman; sculling is a much more individual sport and it is entirely up to the man himself as to how fast he is going to go. This does not apply, to the same extent, to the oarsman rowing in a crew.

Scullers' VIIIs in the Head of the River race have done well and drawn a lot of attention by coming high up the list with few practice outings, yet if one totted up the amount of training done by the individuals concerned it would exceed that of nearly every other crew in the race.

There is no advantage in concentrating on sculling if you

want to win rowing races, and I will go so far as to say that a crew of good oarsmen will always beat a crew of good scullers if they have been trained as hard. My point is that the occasional outing in a sculling boat is very good practice for any oarsman in re-learning the fundamentals of boat-moving.

I have known many distinguished oarsmen who have not been able to scull a stroke but I am certain they would have been even better if they had. Coaches would be well advised to introduce all their crew to sculling, if necessary one or two at a time. If, for instance, there are only two sculling boats available the rest of the crew might split into a four and a pair —the two in the sculls trying out their pace against each other. Then change round the following week.

I am sure that if coaches were prepared to sacrifice, say, one outing in the week to small-boating and sculling the overall standard of their VIIIs would go up far more in proportion than if they were never given the chance to scull at all.

6

The International Class

The rising standard

THE standard of all major sports has been rising steadily throughout the years, with the exception of the period just after the two World Wars when it was generally rather lower than in the immediate pre-war years. This improvement in performance has been unquestioned in those sports where time and distance records have supplied an exact measure of it, but it is still hotly contested by some in sports such as rowing where, owing to the influence of wind and stream, records are suspect. It is true that records have been lowered consistently at Henley Regatta, for instance; but many people, perhaps at a loss to explain whence present-day crews derive their pace, will sooner rely on some hazy impression of great oarsmen and crews of the past, and, because they remember them as rowing so much 'better' than present-day crews, assume that they were faster. On the same basis they would watch E. Zatopek winning a race with his head rolling from side to side—and discount him as being much slower than the graceful athlete of fifty years ago.

Anyone thinking along these lines had better skip this chapter altogether (if indeed they have read so far) because they will not even understand, let alone agree with, what I am about to say. For those who are not so gullible as to believe that there was always a headwind at Henley before the war (in spite of the direction of the flags in some of the old photographs, and statements in the Almanacks), and are prepared to accept that the standard is rising, I am going to attempt an appraisal.

On page 134 below is a table showing the winners of international championships since the war.

I have underlined those crews which came from what are known as the 'Eastern European Countries'. It is noticeable that before 1952 only one such country had won a gold medal —Hungary, in the coxed pairs in 1947. Nineteen-fifty-two saw the emergence of these countries as a major force in rowing, winning twenty gold medals out of an available forty-two in the next five years. This indicates a considerable jump in the standard in 1952, and the reversion that is now taking place is almost certainly due not to a falling off in the standard of the Eastern European crews, but to the countries of the Western *bloc* rising to the challenge.

There is a very good reason for the sudden elevation of the crews of the Communist countries: the official support of their governments, who subsidize not only rowing but most other branches of sport. Oarsmen receive positive encouragement in the following ways:

1. It costs them nothing to row.
2. Jobs can be found convenient to the rowing centre.
3. Centralized training for coaches ensures continuity of method as the oarsmen advance in proficiency.
4. They are released from work at a convenient time to allow them to concentrate on rowing.
5. Medical and other expert knowledge is available at all times.

To combat this members of the Western countries have had to do one or more of the following:

1. Make greater personal sacrifices; for instance, taking an unremunerative job with easy hours, and spending everything on rowing.

Year	Event	Coxed IV	Coxless Pair	Single Sculls	Coxed Pair	Coxless IV	Double Sculls	VIII
1947	E.C.	France	Denmark	France	Hungary	Italy	Holland	Italy
1948	O.G.	U.S.A.	Gt. Britain	Australia	Denmark	Italy	Gt. Britain	U.S.A.
1949	E.C.	Italy	Sweden	U.S.A.	Italy	Italy	Denmark	Italy
1950	E.C.	Denmark	Switzerland	Denmark	Italy	Italy	Denmark	Italy
1951	E.C.	Italy	Belgium	Denmark	Italy	Belgium	Switzerland	Gt. Britain
1952	O.G.	Czechoslovakia	U.S.A.	U.S.S.R.	France	Yugoslavia	Argentina	U.S.A.
1953	E.C.	Czechoslovakia	U.S.S.R.	Yugoslavia	France	Denmark	Switzerland	U.S.S.R.
1954	E.C.	U.S.S.R.	Denmark	Switzerland	Switzerland	Italy	Germany	U.S.S.R.
1955	E.C.	Argentina	U.S.S.R.	Poland	Switzerland	Rumania	U.S.S.R.	U.S.S.R.
1956	E.C.	Finland	U.S.S.R.	U.S.S.R.	Germany	Italy	U.S.S.R.	Czechoslovakia
1956	O.G.	Italy	U.S.A.	U.S.S.R.	U.S.A.	Canada	U.S.S.R.	U.S.A.
1957	E.C.	Germany	Gt. Britain	Australia	Germany	Germany	U.S.S.R.	Italy

E.C.—European Championships.   O.G.—Olympic Games.

2. Devote the whole time to training—but well-to-do parents are a prerequisite.

3. Organize national teams through the auspices of one of the armed services.

4. Sponsoring of teams by large industrial organizations (who do it for publicity value).

5. Organize crews on a university basis with a benevolent staff, possibly financed by a wealthy foundation or group of old students.

6. Produce composite crews from neighbouring rowing clubs.

Anyone who has followed the progress of international rowing in recent years will have little difficulty in recognizing examples from each category.

Whether or not we choose to join in the race, it will undoubtedly continue and the standard is likely to go on improving as it has in the past: as victorious crews of yesterday would be left behind today, so winning crews of today will be superseded by yet faster combinations tomorrow.

Why trouble?

There are those who say that we should not attempt to keep pace with the rising standard and should limit ourselves to purely domestic rowing. They argue that an oarsman can derive full satisfaction from competing against his fellow-countrymen who have practised and trained under similar conditions. To compete against state-aided crews in international competition, having little chance of success, is, they claim, costly and pointless. There are several arguments against this point of view, the most obvious one being that unless we restrict all our regattas to home crews we shall inevitably find ourselves racing some of the best foreign ones, as, for instance, at Henley Regatta, whether we like it or not. To turn away foreign opposition altogether is to lose the opportunity of seeing and learning from the finest crews in the world, while to divide all events into national and international classes would be too humiliating for the majority to tolerate. There is, however, an even more convincing reason for rejecting the 'domestic rowing only' point of view, and that lies with the oarsmen themselves. An oarsman who trains hard and rows well enough to win all his races against British opposition will certainly be looking for new fields to conquer, and so he will be eager to match his pace against the best foreign crews. He is unlikely to be satisfied with the comment that, having beaten all the home opposition, he has reached the top of the tree and should not be allowed to race those from other countries who enjoy better facilities: on the contrary, this will only whet his appetite more.

International rowing brings many rewards to those who achieve sufficient pace to be in the running. Apart from the pleasures to be derived from travelling about the world and meeting fellow-oarsmen of all nationalities there is a certain fascination in competing against crews from all parts of the earth. On one side may be a crew which trains on Moscow River, on the other side one which practises in a harbour in North America, and next to them a crew whose home waters are a Belgian canal. There you are, come from the four corners of the globe to race on the same stretch of water, unable even to speak the same language, but prepared to pit your strength and skill against one another. This element of unfamiliarity and uncertainty has always held a great attraction for me.

Many people deplore the interest that some governments take in the success of their crews in international events, remarking that the sports' arena has become a political stamping-ground where East and West try to prove the merits of their various ideologies, but even if this were so there would be a lot to be said for nations contesting with each other at sporting events rather than with armaments. The foreign oarsmen against whom I have raced have been far from belligerent. Races of three or more crews abreast result in a

PLATE XIV

R.A.F. IV. European Championships, Amsterdam 1954

'. . reached the international standard within a few months.' (page 102)

PLATE XV

Leadley and Davidge winning the Goblets at Henley Royal Regatta, 1957

PLATE XVI

Barn Cottage VIII which won the Head of the River in 1958

PLATE XVII

The author on the towpath when coaching the Oxford University Boat Race
crew in 1958

good deal less individual hostility than is the case in two-abreast races, and it has been my experience that oarsmen from all parts of the world get on remarkably well together considering the tension that inevitably surrounds championships.

Strange as it may seem, it is not the oarsman who takes part in international events who moans about state-sponsored crews and how we should give up competing; nor is it often the crew which loses to the foreigner at Henley that demands that our regattas be closed to competitors from overseas; rather it is the oarsman or coach who is not good enough even to beat his fellow-countrymen, probably because he has set his sights too low in the first place.

Shamateurism

One of the most controversial aspects of modern sport is the question of pseudo-amateurism, or 'shamateurism' as it has been called. This means sportsmen who compete as amateurs but receive help either financially or by being allowed a measure of freedom from work.

There are two obvious sub-divisions in the general category of 'aided amateurs'. Firstly there are the sports clubs which receive gate money from the public and so are able to attract 'amateurs' from other parts of the country with offers of attractive jobs, free housing and so on, all of which infringe the amateur code but are prevalent in both football and cricket and very hard to stop; also, there are the amateurs nominally on the pay-roll of some big firm but free to practise their sport at all times: tennis provides the classic example. Secondly, there are the state-aided amateurs who, though they may not receive definite financial rewards, are nevertheless clothed, fed and housed throughout training as part of a state team. Once sport became a matter of national prestige, with a high-ranking government official to see that all went well, this form of support also became inevitable.

Rowing has escaped from the first category for the simple

reason that there is no money in it and very little spectator attraction, moreover there is no state support whatsoever for sport in this country so that our oarsmen are forced to be true-blue amateurs, whether they like it or not, and no doubt the harsh condemnation of oarsmen from elsewhere who do receive some form of patronage is partly due to a sour grapes attitude on our part. It is all very well to say that a man who is paid a salary and given unlimited opportunities to practise is not an amateur, but cases are rarely as clear-cut as this and I believe that it is quite impossible to draw a dividing line and say at exactly what point true amateurism finishes.

Supposing an internationally famous athlete joins a firm as a salesman, but is given every afternoon free to train. The firm may have employed him purely to help him in his sport, in which case he may be considered a 'shamateur', on the other hand they may have employed him on a part-time basis, in which case he is a true amateur, or they may consider that the fact that he is famous will enable him to sell so much more of their product that they can afford to pay him a day's wage for half a day's work: what is he then?

To take the case of the R.A.F. crews with which I was associated, we did all our training in our spare time until shortly before Henley, when our problem was this: an ordinary airman doing his national service was allowed fourteen days' leave a year, while a three-year man got thirty days and a regular officer forty-two days. We had each type in our crew, and as we had already used up some of our leave competing overseas, in order to spend a fortnight at Henley we either had to throw out all the national service men in the crew, which would have been grossly unfair to them, or to arrange special leave which presumably would have classed them as 'shamateurs'. We always believed in a share-and-share-alike policy with the result that the officers did not use all their leave while the fourteen-day men received rather more than their ration, and I am prepared to defend this attitude vigorously.

The Amateur Rowing Association Rules on the definition of an Amateur are all very nice but nobody takes any notice of them. Rule 3, for example, reads:

No person shall be considered an amateur oarsman, sculler or coxswain who has ever taught, pursued or assisted in the practice of rowing, sculling, or other athletic exercise for any kind of profit.

We included a physical-training instructor in one of our R.A.F. crews; he served in the force, and was paid for the express purpose of teaching in the practice of athletic exercise, yet no one ever queried his entry. Moreover, some men who are schoolmasters at one or other of the rowing schools receive extra remuneration because they are ready to coach the school crews, yet they themselves continue to row and to race in A.R.A. regattas without question. If one checks through the training of those crews which have won international gold medals since the war one makes the discovery that nearly every crew was able to row more frequently than would be possible for normal business men. Winstone and Burnell were double sculling several days a week throughout the winter, and later, Bushnell and Burnell, who won the 1948 Olympic double sculls, were able to devote the whole of the four weeks between Henley and the Olympics to practising. The same year Laurie and Wilson, who were to win the pairs, returned from the Sudan with several weeks of leave which they were able to spend rowing. The Goldie crew, which won the VIII's in the 1951 European Championships, had been able to devote all its time to it since the end of term, in addition to every afternoon for some months before as far as the individuals were concerned. Only Leadley and Davidge (in 1957) were confined to evening and weekend practice and both of them had ten years of top-class rowing behind them.

I quote such cases, not to decry the participants' achievements nor to dishearten those who are tied to an office desk,

but merely to point out that it is difficult to compete successfully in international competition without reasonable facilities
for training. It is pointless to rail against crews who are better
provided for than ourselves and to be shocked and horrified
to discover that the oarsmen in the Polynomian VIII have not
been to work for eight weeks; rather let us learn that we are
not likely to succeed by half measures and that the employer
who believes in keeping his staff late every other evening is best
given a wide berth. As one Russian oarsman replied, when
asked if he actually enjoyed his rowing, 'In Russia every
oarsman wants to row.' There is no shame in spending as much
of one's time on the water as possible, and since the days of
the 'gentlemen of leisure' are over it is necessary to rely to
some extent on the goodwill of one's employer.

Our domestic season

The English rowing season starts around October and extends
throughout the whole of the winter, to finish with the last of
the major summer regattas at the beginning of August. The
European Championships, and frequently the Olympic Games,
are held at the end of August or the beginning of September,
and conclude the international rowing season.

What all too frequently happens is that a crew starts off
somewhat lightheartedly in the autumn and does not become
really serious until after Christmas; during this period there is
a free-and-easy attitude and little continuity of training, with
the result that the keen men find themselves rowing in different
crews from one week to the next. After Christmas the crew
becomes a little more regular and often does some useful long-
distance, stamina-developing rowing up till the Head of the
River race at the end of March. As often as not they then go
completely out of training for three weeks and so undo most
of the good work before starting off, practically from scratch
again, at the end of April. A few weeks' practice and they are
glad to enter for the first regatta to break the monotony of

training; but having had insufficient rowing at a racing pace they usually lose, and then every Saturday for some three months they enter for a regatta. During the week their training will consist of:

Sunday: Day off following Regatta.
Monday: Light outing to get the feel of the boat again.
Tuesday: With luck, a reasonable outing.
Wednesday: Practice starts; row the occasional minute or half-minute.
Thursday: Light outing before Regatta.
Friday: No outing as boat is at Regatta; or first heat at Regatta.
Saturday: Regatta.

If the crew happens to be good enough to win a couple of heats at the early regattas they sometimes achieve sufficient fitness, by dint of racing every Saturday, actually to win an event or two at the end of the season, by which time they are very ready to stop. The idea of aiming at earning international representation, and training to win medals at the European Championships, seldom occurs to them.

In contrast to this a proper approach to the season by, let us say, an VIII should commence with considering what is the main aim—usually either Henley, or Henley and the European Championships or Olympic Games. It is not a bad idea to concentrate on small-boat rowing up until Christmas, alternating the work between sculling (single and double) and pairing, trying at all times to pace the members of the crew against each other. Occasionally the VIII itself may go out, but with the accent generally on individual fitness and skill at this time. After Christmas the VIII should start in earnest: outings as often as possible; plenty of rowing; full four-mile courses from the second weekend onwards, the object at this stage being to win the Head of the River race.

The period immediately after the 'Head' is always a tricky

one; reaction tends to set in and if the crew have done a lot of work in the boat they will need a break of some sort. To do nothing at all is absurd but the answer is now, I think, provided by the Scullers' Head of the River race which follows two weeks later. Every member of the crew who can beg, borrow or steal a boat should enter for it and then set about sculling against one another for the intervening fortnight. Of our R.A.F. VIII, which won the Putney 'Head' in 1954, five entered in the first Scullers' Head and the three in the best boats finished third, fifth and seventh—the only club to get more than one sculler in the first eight. The other two entered in rum-tums and came second and third in that division, one of them actually wearing an old trilby hat and carrying a young boy on the stern canvas.

After the Scullers' Head the VIII should re-form and get down to the all-important job of developing a fast racing gait; eradicating individual faults when a crew is under pressure is a long job and there is no time to waste. May is the vital month and every outing should finish with a flat-out mile course. If the crew are to win at Henley they must be well on the way by the end of May. Entries at regattas must be carefully planned so as to preserve the racing spirit of the crew. I believe that if a crew enters for a regatta every week they may become sick of racing before the end of the season. If members of the crew desperately want to race at the first regattas it will not matter so much entering them in the small-boat events. Sprint races in particular should be treated with caution; if the crew have their eyes on Henley they must learn to be fast over seven minutes and not over four or five—many crews arrive at Henley having rowed few courses over the full distance and this becomes all too obvious during the Regatta between Remenham Club and the Mile. It is always easier to shorten the distance and sprint than vice versa, and even if they do enter for a five-minute race it is better to row all trial courses over seven minutes until the last week.

So far so good; by selecting the events for which one wants to compete it is possible to use the existing domestic season. After Henley, however, things are not arranged with an eye to international championships. Possibly because the colleges have broken up and many of the best crews have stopped rowing the regattas are not in general held over sufficiently long courses and have not attracted many top-class crews; those bent on international representation, however, must continue to race and, as if to acknowledge this fact, the standard of the post-Henley regattas has been rising steadily since the war. National trial races are generally very badly arranged and placed much too near Henley. What is needed is a National Championship regatta held during the first or second week in August over a 2,000-metre course; crews could continue their development throughout the existing season, making any necessary modifications to their composition in the light of the Henley results, and working towards a peak for the National Championships. The winners at this event who were selected for, say, the European Championships would then have about a week to add the final polish before leaving the country.

As things stand at the moment the crew is picked soon after Henley and then has seven weeks before the European Championships. In the meantime they can either compete in open regattas where, if they win, they are called 'pot-hunters', and if they lose everyone starts asking questions; or they need not compete, in which case, unless they are skilfully coached and trained, they arrive at the European Championships short of racing practise. Most crews prefer to play safe and choose the latter course. Anyone who has faced this problem knows what a headache it can be. From the beginning of August every other reasonable crew has given up and an air of complete unreality hovers over practice; the river is deserted and it is hard to retain incentive for what is, necessarily, training for the hardest event of all. Many crews do insufficient work at

143

this time and then travel from the awe-inspiring isolation of rowing in England to the hurly-burly and practice of hundreds of foreign crews—all reaching their climax at the European Championships.

As a national team we were very fortunate in 1954 when the R.A.F. coxless IV, Leander pair and London R.C. double scullers were all training together at Henley and helping each other out in the way of pacing; in the European Championships all three crews reached the finals, two winning medals. But this trouble would never arise if the Amateur Rowing Association were to hold a full-scale National Championship early in August. The reason why the A.R.A. are reluctant to stage a National Championship appears to be twofold. Firstly there is no course in England which matches up to international requirements in providing 2,000 metres of still water with room for four crews abreast. Secondly, an August date is less convenient for the universities; since, however, out of nineteen crews and scullers no undergraduate crew earned selection between 1952 and 1957, except for the Jesus College Cambridge IV in 1955, this does not seem of overriding importance. F.I.S.A. are most unlikely to bring the date of the European Championships forward six weeks so it is up to the A.R.A. to postpone the date of their trials.

The professional coach

It is impossible to consider the improvement necessary in our own national standard without discussing the case for professional coaching, particularly now that this is so prevalent abroad; and the first thing to do is to discount the view that there is something rather unethical about paid coaches. I discussed this once with a member of the 'We don't want to have anything to do with professionals' school of thought. He was convinced that it would lower the standard of amateurism in rowing and was in some way un-English. Yet his Public School employed a famous professional cricketer as coach, his golf club had the services of a 'pro' to advise members, and so did his squash club. It seems incomprehensible to me to accept professional coaching in all other branches of sport and yet to condemn it in rowing.

Every now and again a belated moan echoes round the clubhouse bars, regretting that use has not been made of our great watermen and professional scullers of the past. The reasons have been largely financial, for few clubs have any money to spare, but not many of our excellent professional scullers have had much experience of rowing and I personally have grave doubts whether coaching of this sort would lead to very much of an increase in our standard. Recently one club did have the regular services of an extremely well-known, and one time world professional, sculling champion as coach and the crew that resulted was not at all fast. The best oarsmen do not necessarily make the best coaches or judges of pace, perhaps because their own pace springs from fitness and determination coupled with endless practice in the boat, rather than from a logical examination of all the factors.

When I imagine a professional rowing coach I think rather in terms of the American type: a highly skilled man, perhaps a university graduate, who selects coaching as his profession and makes a life-long study of how to make the most of his material; he needs to be as much a psychologist as a technician. His is the sort of judgement which unerringly selects the eight best boat-movers for the crew—something which no man, amateur or professional, has shown himself capable of doing in this country. To my mind the main advantage of professional coaching lies in continuity: the same man handles the crew throughout the whole of the training period. Because he is paid for it he can give them all his attention whereas here few men are willing, or even able, to spare the time for coaching throughout the season, particularly in the case of Boat Race crews who train every afternoon for at least three months. Some people argue that this is a good thing and that each coach should have his particular function—one to concentrate on individual technique, one to work the crew hard, another to tune them up before the race—but I do not agree. A good coach should be able to do all these jobs, and so avoid the all-too-common occurrence of successive coaches issuing contradictory instructions; everyone has his own concept of the finished article and the crew will develop more quickly if they are taught to a basic theme. The other advantage of a professional is that his career depends, to some extent, upon the class of the crews he turns out. For this reason a poor (quality) coach soon becomes poor (financially) and looks for other work, while men like the head coaches at the big American universities are the very cream of their profession.

As I said earlier there is no money available for clubs to employ full-time coaches, although the major rowing universities could probably manage it. Rather there seems to be a case for encouraging amateurs to gain proficiency and to this end the weekend scheme for coaches, inaugurated by the Amateur Rowing Association in 1957, may, in the long run, prove to be one of the best steps they have taken. It may be possible to develop this idea to the extent of having one or two highly skilled and centrally employed professional coaches who could organize a school as well as visiting rowing centres and giving on-the-spot advice. They would also be invaluable in helping representative crews, but there are obvious snags, the biggest being where to find such professionals.

In the main the future of our international rowing is going to rest with the amateur coach, however much he is aided and abetted by professional advice, and it is worth remembering that the very high standard of Canadian representative crews is the work of one Vancouver business man—Frank Read, himself an amateur, and ardent, coach.

Composite crews

On the face of it there is much to be said for the forming of composite crews to represent the country. Every coach of a successful crew is well aware of one or two members in it whom he would be very ready to replace if given the chance to name anyone else he preferred. So it seems logical to pick upon a successful crew as a basis and strengthen it where required, if not to build a new crew from scratch. There have been many examples of fast composite crews, for instance the legendary Belgian crews of 1906, 1907 and 1909 which won the Grand, and the recent Swedish VIII hailing from the 'Three Towns' —Kungslav, Stromstad and Trollhatten.

Composite crews are very unpopular at the moment for the simple reason that the two examples of crews picked on form to represent the country since the war were outstanding failures. The first of these, the Empire Games VIII of 1950, were beaten by both Australia and New Zealand by four lengths, and the 1956 Olympic VIII suffered the same fate by the same margin at the hands of America, Canada and Australia. The two cases were, however, rather different; in 1950 the oarsmen chosen had distinguished themselves in open and international events, all but one having won the Grand in the two previous years, and while their failure could be put down to insufficient practice, interrupted coaching and a run of bad luck in losing both boat and riggers in transit, few could have argued over the men selected. The case of the 1956 Olympic crew was undoubtedly the most disastrous attempt ever made in this country. Nothing was done at all until after Henley when a crew was hastily collected together for the European Championships. Few of the oarsmen chosen had distinguished themselves in open competition, and as the crew was subsequently coached by men who had not been consulted over the selection there was little continuity or cohesion. When the VIII, somewhat altered, finally left to compete in Melbourne it is doubtful whether it would have won the Thames

Cup at Henley. It is not surprising that the case for composite crews was completely shattered; even the oarsmen concerned were at pains to produce a manifesto demanding that in future trial races be held.

Yet because the selectors in those years were unable to judge merit it does not follow that composite crews are necessarily wrong or bound to fail. Assuming that several clubs wish to combine to put out a composite crew, it is imperative that selection and coaching are planned well in advance by the same people so that successive coaches do not alter the crew or use conflicting systems. Similarly, it is essential that the oarsmen concerned are all prepared to work together with the coach to produce a fast crew.

In the absence of National Trials, and if no individual crew has shown itself, at Henley, to be fast enough to represent the country, so that it is necessary to turn out a composite national crew at short notice, one of the best ideas that I have heard is roughly this: the four most successful coaches are seeded by the selectors in order of merit, let us say A, B, C and D. Coach A is then allowed to select his crew from all the available material (assumed to be fit and have raced recently) and, when he is finished, coach B takes his pick from the remainder and so on until each coach has chosen his crew. They are then given a period of, say, three or four weeks in which to train their crews, when a race is held over 2,000 metres. Suppose C's crew wins, coach C is then appointed as national coach and he can select whoever he likes to make up the national crew. He might take his original crew but more than likely he will want to make further trials and perhaps strengthen it by bringing in, say, two oarsmen out of A's and one out of B's. This method ensures that the final coach chosen is either a very good selector or a very good coach or both; in any case, he will have confidence in the crew and they will have good reason to trust his judgement and ability. Difficulties may arise owing to the widely separated rowing centres in this country, but it might be possible to modify this scheme by having one composite crew from each centre, say one from Oxford, one from Cambridge and one from the Tideway clubs. Moreover, if any other coach feels that he can raise a crew to beat all the others (from the oarsmen left) there is no reason why he should not enter it in the final trial races, the same rules applying—if his crew wins he has *carte blanche* to produce the national crew.

One final word. There is no room for sentiment in top-class rowing; however hard a man may have trained, however set he is on being selected, if another oarsman is available who is a better boat-pusher he should be in and the first man out. Let me say that in producing British crews for which I have been responsible I have never hesitated to bring in stronger men if they were available, despite the criticism which this has aroused. As an example, in 1953 we exchanged the stroke of our record-breaking Wyfold IV after we had been selected for the European Championships. J. W. Johnson had stroked our VIII and IV at Henley to win ten races in the four days—a magnificent effort which had nevertheless destroyed the edge to his rowing. Davidge, as coach, and I, as captain, talked it over and as a result we brought in G. Sorrell after we had been selected because we considered that he would make the crew faster, and I am certain we were justified in this decision. International competition is very exacting and—as I said before —there is no room for sentiment.

The way ahead

Too much of the criticism levelled against present-day British crews is destructive and too much of it emanates from men who have not taken the trouble to examine the background to world-beating crews. Above all I intend to try and be constructive over the all-important question of raising the standard of our rowing.

Let us realize what we are up against. Today there are between thirty and forty countries taking part in international championships; excluding the coxed pairs, for which we do not enter, there are six events left—VIIIs, coxed and coxless IVs, pairs, double sculls and single sculls. Three medals are awarded for each event—gold, silver and bronze, which means that our crews have to compete against the best of thirty other nations for a total of eighteen medals. If one balances the stronger rowing countries, such as Russia and America, against the weaker ones, it is obvious that numerically the odds are against a British crew bringing back a medal at all. The dice are heavily loaded against winning a gold medal. In 1954 the R.A.F. had the good fortune to win the silver medal for the coxless IVs at the European Championships at Amsterdam; although we would much sooner have come first, we considered that we had done pretty well, but when we returned people consoled us with such remarks as 'Hard luck!' and 'Why did you lose?' In addition, Macklin and Davidge won the bronze medal for the coxless pairs and Fox and Marsden were fourth in the double sculls, yet the *Rowing Almanack*, commenting on a poor season, remarked that 'the fact remains that we were unable to win one gold medal'.

Observations such as this indicate a fundamental lack of comprehension of the standard involved and of the odds against coming first—of twenty countries competing in 1954, fifteen went home without any gold medals. Those who watched the final of the VIIIs at Ghent in 1955 and saw the Swedish crew run a close second to Russia, after being last of four by some lengths at halfway, will remember them throwing their arms in the air and congratulating each other on coming second when, if the course had been a fraction longer, they might well have won. This suggests an entirely different approach. Some people glibly talk of our crews not being up to international standard because they did not get to the final of the European Championships or Olympic Games, but no one defines what this standard is. Each crew that represents its country is the best from that country and collectively they form the international standard. If a British crew can compete on equal terms with such crews and beat some of them it must be of international standard; to condemn it for failing to beat most or all of the other countries is profitless, and very disheartening for the men concerned.

The results show that in many cases the gold medal winners are oarsmen who have, so to speak, been knocking on the door for years. One case that has already been mentioned was that of the Rumanian coxless IV, which failed to reach even the semi-finals in the 1954 European Championships, but won the gold medal the following year; if it had been a British crew it would probably have been written off after 1954 as 'not up to international standard'. An outstanding case of persistence was that of T. Kocerka, the Polish sculler, whose record reads: 1952 Olympics, third; 1953 European Championships, second; 1954 European Championships, second; and finally 1955 European Championships—first! The purpose of relating these facts is to emphasize how years of less successful racing in international events can build up one's knowledge and experience until a win becomes possible. If the point needs further stressing remember that C. G. V. Davidge, stroke of the gold medal pair in the 1957 European Championships (and our only win in the post-1952 era), had already contested that event in 1952 (O.G.), 1954 (E.C.) and 1956 (E.C.).

If success is achieved by learning more and more about modern international rowing it follows that no good can be served by copying methods that were only good enough to beat the standard of thirty years ago.

It is, however, interesting to note the training that was done by the veteran VIII which won the 1908 Olympics as recorded by Guy Nickalls in *Life's a Pudding*: 'We paddled in one piece from Putney to Kew Bridge, and rowed and paddled alternatively [alternately?] all the way home in one piece no matter which way or how fast the tide was running or what was the state of the tide.' They did this every night for five days a week and the distance involved is exactly eleven miles—here at least is something which the Tideway clubs would do well to copy.

Coming back to my original three S's—Strength, Stamina and Skill—it appears that we could do with attracting more big, strong men to the sport. Far too often they are neglected because they upset the boat and are clumsy in their movements, and because coaches are unwilling to spend the time and trouble in helping them they are replaced by smaller, neater men who make the boat initially faster. I remember watching the German coxed IV winning in Duisburg in 1957. They came lumbering up the course in the final, rowing at about 36; individually and collectively they were committing dozens of faults of technique and yet they won. I was standing by the boathouse when they came ashore and as they walked past me I realized how enormous they were—average height must have been about 6 ft. 4 in. They were just bigger and stronger than their opponents.

Few men in this country have any conception of how badly undertrained our crews are by international standards. I have in front of me a copy of the magazine *Rowing* (Vol. III, No. 60) in which the Oxford University correspondent writes: 'It seems that in England generally, and this is certainly the case at Oxford, too much emphasis is placed on fitness at the expense of oarsmanship.' This is a misconception that is far too prevalent today and is propagated by people who have no idea whatsoever what training is done by winning Olympic crews. I should say that the emphasis on oarsmanship, as opposed to the development of racing stamina, was many times greater than it should have been at Oxford at the time this piece was written. Perhaps as a result of the annual Boat Race hysteria British oarsmen are scared of doing much work in the boat for fear of 'going over the top'; with few exceptions they all fail because they never really get going at all.

Let me relate the training done by the University of

British Columbia VIII and IV which won silver and gold medals in the 1956 Olympics. They were nearly all in their first or second year of rowing; the IV in particular were all novices. In the last six and a half months they covered some 4,000 miles in training. To do this they would get up at 4.30 a.m. and be on the water by 5.30, when they would row some eight to ten miles; in the evening they would cover another ten to twelve miles; at intervals they would include thirty-mile outings.

Each outing would consist of paddling in three- to five-mile stretches, the rate being about 24 during the first three months, working up to 28 to 30 during the last three. At the end of every outing, that is, twice a day, they would row a flat-out 2,000-metre course.

For each piece of work the IV would be sent out in front and told to stay there as long as they could.

When they arrived at Melbourne the IV, having always started ahead of the VIII in practice, had no idea of how to do a racing start and consequently they were always led; however, once they got into their economical gait of 34 their pace was so great that they swept past all the opposition and in the second half of the course were quite unchallenged. (This IV subsequently rowed in the Canadian VIII—shown in Plate VII—which won the Empire Games in 1958. The IV was made up of 2, 3, 5 and Stroke of this VIII.)

If this does not point to success achieved by inexperienced oarsmen through the rapid build-up of strength and stamina at high ratings and mileage under pressure, then I do not know what does.

By contrast, consider the training done by the American coxed and coxless pairs which both won at Melbourne. Every evening they would go out together and paddle at 28–30 for fifteen minutes, rowing every stroke as hard as possible, stop and turn round, come back for six minutes doing the same thing and then finish with a flat-out 2,000-metre course. Although they would only cover six miles and be back within the hour the intensity with which they did all their work amply made up for its brevity.

Finally, skill. I believe that improved technique will not raise our standard by more than a small fraction of that required to win medals at international events, but there are two failings which are almost universal in our rowing today. First of all, our crews do not use their legs throughout the stroke because they kick their slides away on the beginning, their blades not being locked in the water; this means that the legs are not doing nearly enough work in relation to the other muscle groups, and that the impetus towards the bows checks the boat. Secondly, far too many crews partly feather under water at the finish and let the run of the boat take their blades out for them, instead of rowing them out squared and feathering them as they come on to the balance. To some extent I think this fault arises from the current trend towards stiffer and stiffer oars. To row a 'square' finish with a rigid oar requires immense quickness and co-ordination which are generally lacking at the end of a hard row.

In British rowing what is needed most is a realization of what is required to win international events, and basically that is a fanatical desire to win races at all costs. Our crews are much too occupied in other ways to worry about this: they want to look fast, to earn praise from their old members or from the Press on the way that they row, and to row comfortable trial courses—so they avoid doing them when conditions are poor; for the same reason few crews trouble to row themselves out completely in practice, because when a crew is rowed out it becomes ragged.

From my experience at international championships I should say that about half the British crews at Henley are rowing technically well enough to win medals if they would only take the trouble to train properly. But they never realize this, everyone telling them how badly they were rowing when they were beaten. What they are never told is that they were rowing badly mainly because they had never done sufficient training at a flat-out rowing rate. Yet if a crew does take the trouble to do a reasonable amount of training it earns the grudging praise that it only won because it was so fit, as if this were cheating in some way.

My advice to any group of oarsmen really wanting to win big races is to get some enthusiastic and honest man to act as coach; set about training on similar lines to that employed by world-beating crews; take no notice whatsoever of adverse criticism; and no matter who you race or what standard you reach—row to win!

Index